From
Gloom
&
Glitz
Glory
to

From Gloom & Glitz *to* Glory

He Heard Me Weep

Dr. Edna M. Sullivan, DM

Library of Congress Control Number:		2014907714
ISBN:	Hardcover	978-1-4990-0807-4
	Softcover	978-1-4990-0808-1
	eBook	978-1-4990-0798-5

ESV—English Standard Version

Scripture taken from The Holy Bible, English Standard Version® (ESV®), copyright © 2001 by Crossway, a publishing ministry of Good News Publishers. Used by permission. All rights reserved.

KJV—King James Version

Scripture taken from the King James Version of the Bible.

NASB—New American Standard Bible

Scripture taken from the New American Standard Bible®, Copyright © 1960, 1962, 1963, 1968, 1971, 1972, 1973, 1975, 1977, 1995 by The Lockman Foundation. Used by permission." (www.Lockman.org)

NIV—New International Version

Scripture taken from the Holy Bible, New International Version®. Copyright © 1973, 1978, 1984 Biblica. Used by permission of Zondervan. All rights reserved.

This book was printed in the United States of America.

Rev. date: 07/25/2014

To order additional copies of this book, contact:
Xlibris LLC
1-888-795-4274
www.Xlibris.com
Orders@Xlibris.com
552411

Table of Contents

Acknowledgements

Thank you Father, I appreciate You and praise your Holy Name. Your awesomeness love is immeasurable. You are my *joy* and the *glory* of my life! Thank you, for being present and involved in my life from the beginning until now. Your loving protection and guidance, allowed me to forgive myself of doubt and sins committed prior to learning how to be submissive to your Word. Please, restore those who I may have mislead in my ignorance. I regret many mistakes of my past. I'm grateful to you for having *mercy* on me. Thank you for allowing me to go through heartache, pain, and despair, so I could be molded and become solely dependent on you. Thank you for transforming me each day.

Many wonderful people have contributed in immeasurable ways to my experience of writing this book. My gratitude goes to my family, who generously shared me for many long hours while I wrote this manuscript. I will always be grateful and appreciative of your love and support. I especially want to thank my daughter, Zina Cooper and son-in-law Calvin Cooper, and my sisters, Cheryl Brack and Jackie Calabrese, for every hour spent praying and encouraging me to be consistent in my quest. I also want to acknowledge my church families in Ohio and Georgia.

Thank you, Mrs. Rosie Ivery Pettygrue, my third grade teacher and God-given friend, who has contributed to this project and has always encouraged me to work hard. You have significantly impacted this book and my life. Your vote of confidence has not only encouraged me but challenged me to delve more deeply into prayer.

Dr. Mark Baggit, although we've known each other for a short period, your support and inspiring words truly motivated me to keep going on.

Thank you, Les Roberts, for your enthusiasm and introducing me to the world of writing. Meeting you and reading your novels inspired me to read as many books as I could and to share my story of hope to touch the lives of others.

Everyone should have an editor like Angela Jackson, who allowed me to share a story of hope not horror. You, made sure my words were expressed with Christian dignity. The countless hours of careful typing, restructuring, and formatting is much appreciated. You are truly a blessing.

Special thanks to, Senior Pastor Jeff Greer and the Riverchase Baptist Church family, who treated me and my work with dignity and integrity. And lastly my gratitude extends to my dear friends Pastor and Mrs. George Adams and my best friend Dr. Jose A. Gotay.

Chapter 1

The Faith Principle

Have you waited on God for something so long that you've become unsure of His promises? Maybe, you landed at the wrong church and bad experiences with believed Christians nearly stopped you from finding another church home altogether. Perhaps, you loved someone so deeply and your heart was broken so your refuse to give it another try. Possibly, family abuse and rejection made you flee your hometown with no desire to return. By chance, high-stress times have you ready to throw in the towel on life. Or, is it that your child has decided to pick gang life over family values. Whatever the fear, circumstance or difficulty, think about what saved you through the storms of life. If we look back over our lives, we will find that we are never alone. God has a plan for our lives. He works "behind the scenes" to help us complete our mission. Release your faith by asking and believing it will come to pass in His perfect timing.

In all my years of living and over 30 years in ministry, I've come to learn the more we become like Him in our character, Satan seeks control of two things – our thoughts and our hearts. Too often today, when "the going gets tough" the desire to hate, run, hide, cheat and quit overrules the mind. By building a stronger relationship with God, we become better equipped to resist the Devil's wiles. God wants us to know Him. Through study, fellowship, and service we can sharpen our discernment and walk in faith.

In my youth, some people, considered me as a "frisky little girl" who only thought of prancing and dancing. In other words, they thought I was "fast" as it was called then. My questionable behavior was largely due to how I felt deep inside. Some days, I felt so unloved and lonely that I thought the world would be a much better place without me in it. "Give up!" often crossed my mind. Yet, I was too afraid to follow through with "ending it all" or proceeding with another escape plan. Outright failure of either would simply make my inadequacies stand out to those I longed so hard to please; especially, Mrs. Gertrude. With time, God placed a stronger desire to survive in my thoughts, attitudes, and words.

We must learn to trust His promises. Through good times and bad, God's love for us doesn't change. Life is a time of preparation. Many lessons are taught at different times and under different circumstances. The times, I felt ready to find out exactly what "Rest In Peace" really meant made me wonder if I was being punished by God. After all, He knows everything and surely how my life came into existence. Satan's weapons were at work. Thoughts of being called "ugly" and "fast" raced through my mind. Along with, "Go ahead, run away. RIP!"

Today, many of His children are still exposed to forms of emotional, physical, and sexual abuse. These young lives often struggle with feelings of fear, anger, self-blame, and thoughts of suicide. A "temporary escape" from the overwhelming sense of unworthiness is often found in drugs, alcohol, eating, sexting, cyber-bullying, and gambling. As they struggle to find happiness and love, ministers, church members, schools, and many other legal, social, and charitable organizations search for solutions to help.

The Anatomy of Giving Up

Why do people give up when things get complicated? What's missing from one's life that they are willing to call it quits? Where can one find hope? Author and Gallop Senior Scientist, Shane J. Lopez (2013) views "hope" as oxygen. We cannot live without oxygen. Lopez (2013) implied that hope is the "head and heart combined" and includes emotions such as joy, respect, and excitement. He compared "wishing" and "hoping." He stated to distinguish a wish from a hope is sometimes complicated because, "wishing is 'future think' that sparks no action. Only hope starts an individual thinking about ways to make life better and gets them moving." (Lopez, 2013, p. 20). Lopez stated that "hope is contagious." It is something good that can be spread from one person to another. He was referring to the hope of individuals in a learning environment. However, the message assumes that any person who lacks perseverance also lacks hope, and the willpower to survive. In the article, *Making Hope Happen in the Classroom*, Lopez identified three features drawn from his research of students around the world. Lopez implied the trio of characteristics attributed to why some students are more successful than others.

First, hopeful students have a reason to hope. The content rarely matters and can range from a family outing, sporting event, or a school dance as long as it is something that energizes the student. The student's enthusiasm is created and sustained by the high expectation of what the future will bring. In the same way, a Christian waits with enthusiasm for God's promises.

Second, a hopeful student has a mind to keep going. Lopez (2013) discovered that absenteeism is one of the biggest problems in America's schools today. He and his colleagues measured the hope of students entering the ninth grade and followed them periodically. The discovery was made that students with "high hope" missed only two days of school during the first term, but students with "low hope" missed twice as much. The Bible tells us to "be steadfast, immovable, always abounding" knowing that we will be rewarded in the end (Corinthians 15:58).

Third, a hopeful student displays an attitude of belief. This student is psychologically invested in the process of learning. He or she becomes actively engaged in participating. The Gallop Student Poll revealed, nearly three out of four students who were hopeful about school were also hopeful about the future. Their spirits are lifted and they are energized by the joy of knowing that in some mysterious way the hard work and suffering is worth it. Christians are encouraged to "not grow weary of doing what is good; for if we don't give up, we will in due time reap the harvest" (Galatians 6:9).

The Essential Role of Hope

What is hope? *Merriam-Webster Dictionary* defines the word as an intransitive verb meaning, "to cherish a desire with anticipation." As an archaic verb, meaning to "trust." and, a transitive verb meaning "to desire with expectation of obtainment" and "to expect with confidence." The biblical definition of hope is "confident expectation." Hope is a firm assurance regarding things that are unclear and unknown (Romans 8:24-25; Hebrews 11:1, 7). Hope is a fundamental part of the life of the righteous (Proverbs 23:18).

Many of us can relate to hope in the same way we anticipate events happening in our lives. Those in love have waited for marriage proposals from that special someone. Children have hoped for desired gifts at Christmastime. Sports fans have cheered on their favorite teams. Throughout our lives, we wait and hope for circumstances and events to occur. Waiting means anticipation and expectation. God is waiting to "show out" in our lives when we seek His guidance.

"Hope and Change" was a campaign slogan in the 2008 presidential election. The hope of having Barak Obama elected as the first black president of the United States of America bought many voters to the polls. Through "hope" and "change" he even landed a second term at the dismay of some. Hope is a major factor throughout the lifetime of every living being. From birth to adulthood, we hope for physical, mental, emotional, and financial success. With faith and hope we can persevere against all odds

Emphasis on the Future

Hope is a high expectation that something we anticipate happening will take place. Both, Biblical hope and human hope focus on something happening in the future. Imagine, waiting for your favorite TV show. Whether, you indulge in watching *The Real Housewives of Atlanta, Scandal, Criminal Minds* or the *Evening News* you've had to wait for it to broadcast. Many people are so fascinated with "distorted pictures of the truth" they impatiently wait for the arrival of its programming date and time or make sure to DVR so they won't miss a beat. Some people are so consumed with their TV faves that a Presidential Address or Sports Bowl interruption becomes annoying. Religious broadcasting is of importance to many Christians who eagerly wait for their favorite talk shows, messaging or online shopping program too. Just as we find comfort and direction in TV faves, we must not fail to show the same anticipation and excitement concerning God's plan for us.

As Christians, we must turn to the Scriptures and learn how to get excited about what He has in store for us. Since the Israelites had faith in God's provision; they were saved from Pharaoh's army. Faith is sure of something, even though we cannot see it (Hebrews 11:1). Waiting on God, requires activation of our faith. Though we cannot authorize a release of the gift of faith ourselves, God through His loving kindness and mercy causes our faith to increase.

Emphasis on a Fact

When we realize that God has given us everything essential to our lives then we shall be complete. When God sent down perfection through Jesus Christ and the Holy Spirit he gave us faith, grace, salvation, and eternal life just for the asking.

> *"For God did not appoint us to suffer wrath but to receive salvation through our Lord Jesus Christ. He died for us so that, whether we are awake or asleep, we may live together with him"* (1 Thessalonians 5:9-10).

Our lives are essentially built upon the foundation of hope. If we have hope, we can endure. However, hope is on every Christian's "most wanted" list. Hope gives us the motivation we need to continue when quitting is so easy to do. Hope gives us the vitality to keep going when we are at our weakest point, and hope is the "necessary part" that keeps us trusting and believing in God's promise of a victorious outcome.

Faithful People in My Life

I have been privileged throughout my life and as a minister to see many people who are examples of hope. Throughout the pages of this book, you'll meet these blessed souls who have provided me with a wealth of knowledge. Their actions have assured me that they're destined to spend eternity with the King of Kings.

Deborah, a faithful Pastor's wife was diagnosed with a rare form of terminal cancer. She didn't give in to the frightening news of her medical condition. Instead, she became more vigilant as a servant to the Lord. Her service to members of the church and the community compounded with her hope and trust in God sustains her today.

James, who lost both parents and a sister to cancer, found out later that he also was stricken with the disease. He too, didn't let the frightening news of his medical condition hinder his devout service to the prison ministry or faith in God. James has remained hopeful and is expecting the miracle of healing.

Kim, found at the prime of her life she had a life threatening illness that required major surgery. Through her faith in God, she remained hopeful, gathering information about the disease, and educating others on living healthier lives.

Mable faithfully served the Lord. She lost her job of 25 years and struggled to survive. She has since earned a high-ranking position with a flexible scheduling that allows her the time off to attend both, church and Bible College.

Cathy, lost hope in life. She was physically and emotionally abused by a family member throughout her childhood. Clinging to faith helped her regain hope for the future. She is now an advocate for abused children in her community.

Each of these individuals is living examples of hope in what possibly seemed as hopeless situations. It brings to mind, some of the questions Job asked, "What strength do I have, that I should still hope? What prospects, that I should be patient?" (Job 6:11, NIV). Then I realize that the answer is in Jesus. 1 Thessalonians states, "We remember before our God and Father your work produced by faith, your labor prompted by love, and your endurance inspired by hope in our Lord Jesus Christ" (1 Thessalonians 1:3, NIV). Without hope we have nothing.

Relatives of Hope

Upon an initial visit to a doctor's appointment, you are usually asked to provide your medical history. Providing medical information about your parents, grandparents, and siblings helps determine your likelihood of developing the same or similar medical issues. Relatives of hope include the following key elements:

Waiting

Waiting is an important principal of hope. Most people hate to wait. One of the most difficult challenges in life is waiting. However, learning to wait can be accomplished. We dislike sitting in the waiting rooms, checkout lines in stores, lines to board a plane, or other things that might delay us getting what we want, when we want it.

One of the greatest lessons we can learn is to wait. Through waiting, we will discover the purpose God has for us. "The Lord is good to those who wait for Him, to the person who seeks Him" (Lamentations 3:25). The energy and power we need to survive will be given by the Lord. Isaiah 40:20-31, gives us the assurance of receiving supernatural restoration from God. Proverbs 20:22 let us know that our victory is assured by God. Therefore, we do not repay evil, God has full control.

Those who "wait" will realize the fulfillment of our faith according to Isaiah 49:23. And, they will not be put to disgrace because of their faithfulness. Each who remains faithful "will receive his commendation from God" (1 Cor. 4:5). If we remain faithful and wait (Isaiah 64:4) we will see God working on our behalf.

Endurance

Throughout this book we will see statements significant to hope. We will follow and discuss the lives of many people who endured through trials and stressful situations. Paul prayed that Christians would be strengthened with "God power" to have strong endurance and patience. We need that same endurance accompanied by our joyful appreciation. Paul challenged the disciples (2 Timothy 2:3) to share in hardships and suffering and to expect hardships to come.

We must endure because failure to do so in marriage, work, church, or any area of life would deem us defeated by the sin of disobedience. Our instructions have already been provided in God's Word, calling for us to follow Him and to endure for His glory. Endurance takes more than a desire to make something work, endurance means being transformed. The Scripture speaks of this in 2 Corinthians 3:18.

One of the most important concepts of the Bible is that of withstanding life's test. The Latin translation of word endurance is *patientia* meaning patience, suffering, and endurance. When I looked up the word endurance in *The NAS New Testament Greek Lexicon*, I discovered the word *hupomone* which the NAS uses 32 times (Thayer & Smith, 1999). In this edition, the Greek translation *hupomone* is similar meaning steadfastness, constancy, and endurance and was referred to endurance 7 times. The word endurance is mentioned many places in the Scriptures, suggesting how essential it is in our lives. Romans 5:3-4, encourages to rejoice in our sorrows because sorrows produce endurance and endurance produces character which leads to hope.

Contentment

Contentment is proof of a Christian's true faith and profession to Christ. A true Christian realizes that his or her life is a creation of God, by God, and for God's glory. Contentment is to therefore, what Paul stated in Philippians 4, "I have all that I need in Christ Jesus." A Christian can also say, I lack for nothing because "the Lord is my portion" (Psalms 119). To be content is to be truly happy and satisfied in belonging to God.

Paul's attitude while in prison was that of a content man. Thou he was imprisoned and chained to soldiers on both sides, he remained faithful to God. He knew that God was with through all of his trials which gave him strength to endure. By faith, Paul was united with Christ. The Lord was "with" Paul and "in" Paul. The following verses, provide further insight on the meaning of contentment: Philippians 4:11-13; 1 Timothy 6:6-11; 2 Corinthians 12:9-10; Romans 8:28; Job 36:11 and Proverbs 19:23.

Confidence

It wasn't until I became a parent and was faced with the intensity of enduring the many decisions and challenges of my children that I understood what confidence really meant. I came to realize my faults, weaknesses, and shortcomings and became convicted by the way they affected my children.

Over 33 years ago, my friend Gloria's son was molested by a trusted man in the community. She was a young, single parent trying to work two or three jobs to care for her children so they wouldn't have to suffer or want for anything. While what they really ended up needing most was "their mother." Getting your children involved in community centers and youth clubs was thought to be the best outlet for building character. However, the opposite was true for Gloria's son. During their time in the care of others, her children received more harm than they should have and their wait for a new toy or going to private school could make it up.

Gloria's son Jason was always a very happy and smart child. But, became somewhat secluded and preoccupied with G.I. Joe and battle toys after the age of 12. She was too busy to realize what her child was going through. He was suffering mentally and emotionally. He was afraid. Jason began skipping classes and hiding out at home whenever he could get away with it. He went through the anguish and fears all alone and had become very angry. School and every other aspect of life became a challenge for him.

I will never forget where I was or what I was doing the day I received the phone call from Gloria that Jason had been suspended from school. I was standing in the principal's office at the school where I worked talking to my friend and co-worker when the call came to his phone. He said, "She's right here." With deep astonishment, I wondered who could be calling me and what had taken place. It was Gloria calling to tell me that the school principal had called to tell her that Jason had used his shop tools to create a sharp object that could be harmful to other people. I almost fainted, not knowing the nature of the call. That was the moment I began to associate Jason's mental limitations with God's power.

I left work early to go to the aid of my friend and I prayed all the way to the school, asking God to give me the strength and the right words to say to her in this situation. I was also a single parent and had a feeling of the fear she was having. She had too much on her mind to be angry with Him or to realize Satan was trying to take something very precious from her. Her self-confidence was shattered and her thoughts were; had I failed as a mother? Was I losing control of my child? Gloria even wondered if she was being punished for divorcing her children's father.

This profound revelation this could be nearly blew me away. When I arrived at the school, Gloria was composed and able to talk calmly to both school authorities and her son. God had sheltered her thoughts and emotions and protected her during a time when she needed Him most. Her love for the Lord never failed but her self-confidence had. She knew that the One who created her was stronger than her fears and struggles. Her strength even gave me courage and I remembered what Deuteronomy said about being courageous, "Be strong and courageous. Do not be afraid or terrified because of them, for the Lord your God goes with you; he will never leave you nor forsake you" (Deuteronomy 31:6, NIV).

Philippians helps us to see what having confidence in God really means. Confidence in God supernaturally strengthens us, energizes us, and empowers us to accomplish and receive all that God sets before us. It is through confidence in God that fear and doubt is replaced by the blessed assurance that God will do what is best for His children. Whenever you feel yourself losing faith, call on God. Philippians 4:5, assures us that "The Lord is near."

God's care for us is endless. He will never be far from the reach of His children. He promises that he will never leave or forsake us. His watchful eye is forever protecting and overseeing our actions. Philippians 4:7 states, "And the peace of God will guard your heart and your minds." The Lord will provide peace for our hearts and mind. God knows those who love His son and allows him to live inside of them. He will watch over, protect, and care for them. Philippians 4:13 states, "I can do all things through Him who strengthens me." Today, Gloria's son is a Christian, has earned a Master's degree in social work and is the proud grandfather of four.

A Positive Picture of Faith and Hope

One of the most positive and confident individuals I've met in my life is my third grade teacher, Rosie Ivery Pettygrue. Mrs. Rosie is one of the most respected and highly honored educators from Eastern Kentucky. I recall our many conversations that not only inspired me but also served as my guiding light.

When I first met Ms. Rosie, I was a frightened 8-year-old little girl entering the third grade. The first thing she said to the class was "come on in here you children and find a seat. We will make assignments later." Then she looked at me and said, "You sit right here!" I guess she could see how afraid I was. The attention she gave us helped us to comfortably settle into our new routines. I didn't know at the time that this was her first teaching job. She was 20-years-old, fresh out of college, single with no family in town. Perhaps, she was a little scared on this first day of school also. Other than her boss, his family, and a few people she met at Kentucky State University she didn't know many people in this part of Kentucky. She often said, "One comforting thing is my Eastern Kentucky friends could really cook." They invited her over for dinner on a regular basis.

Throughout my youth, Ms. Rosie motivated and encouraged students like myself to be the best that we could be. She even reminded me how beautiful and special I was to her and God. The most important thing Ms. Rosie shared with me was at some point in life, everyone will experience things that might make them sad. However, we have power within to overcome such matters. She taught me how to replace feelings of hopelessness with hope.

No Regrets

Ms. Rosie eventually became Mrs. Rosie. I was thrilled when the retired educator, agreed to let me interview her for this book. One afternoon, she called and said "Okay, I'm ready." Our conversation began with me asking, "Can you tell me about yourself, please?" Her smile came through the phone as she spoke. It didn't take long to realize, her family means the world to her.

Ms. Rosie met the love of her life, Ernest, during her first year residing in Lynch, Kentucky. Mrs. Rosie Ivery Pettygrue has been married for over 55 years now. She is also the proud mother of two adult daughters and three grandchildren. Mrs. Rosie was surprised but happy to learn of the "driving role" she has played in my life. She motivated me to go further than I ever imagined. With her guidance and words of encouragement I went from being a nervous little girl with low self-esteem to a woman who doesn't accept failure as an option.

When asking, "What does family mean to you?" Mrs. Rosie said, "Everything!" She went on to explain, "A bad family is better than no family at all!" Over the years, I have noticed from the hundreds of students I've taught that children are always trying to find a connection for growth and development. It doesn't matter whether they're adopted or foster children, they want to know something about family." Her speaking of connections allowed me to easily probe further.

"Why did you decide to become a teacher?" I inquired. "During the time I was going to school, the only professions "people of color" were pursuing were, nursing, teaching, and secretarial," Mrs. Rosie said. She chose teaching because both of her parents were educators. Plus, she was drawn to sharing knowledge. Her love of teaching little children in day care, in addition to her early years of babysitting, and the experiences enjoyed in student teaching motivated her to teach. "It was just something I always enjoyed," she explained.

When asked to describe her teaching philosophy. Mrs. Rosie responded by saying, "The best philosophy I have is to know something about who you are teaching. Know about their culture and try to understand their spiritual affiliation. This helps you manage in diverse classroom structures." She then stated, "I brought versatility to my classes by involving the students and allowing them to share rather than have them always listen to me. I allowed myself to learn from them, just as they learned from me." She went on to say, "I learned in college the importance of learning to do by doing."

As my questions came to a close, Mrs. Rosie addressed even a higher calling when asked, "Are you a Christian? Do you believe teaching is one of the highest callings from God? And, how do you help children build self-esteem?" Her answers were, "Yes I am a Christian. I was raised in a Christian home and have been very active in church all of my life. I do believe 'teaching is a calling' and you have to love it or you will not do well at it. I loved teaching and using different strategies to help students learn. Vacation Bible School and babysitting some of my professor's children at Kentucky State helped me to realize I had chosen the right field. You must show that you care and that the children you are teaching are important to you and to their community. This builds self-esteem," she shared.

I asked Mrs. Rosie a final question, "Do you believe that you've helped to improve the self-esteem of any of her students?" She said, "I believe I have and I feel blessed when students I have taught come back and say Mrs. Pettygrue you helped me or I am where I am today because you went over and above to help me. Attorney Charles White of Indiana and you are two students I am very proud of. There are many others who let me know that I did what God created me to do. The many invitations, cards, and acknowledgements from students and their parents keep me smiling. I have no regrets about the path God has chosen for me."

Rosie has motivated many individuals to gain as much knowledge as possible even in her late 70s; she continues to provide guidance and instructions to both younger and older people. In a future book, I will explain to you the hope this woman Rosie Ivery Pettygrue had as a first time black graduate student in an all-white college in the hills of Kentucky. Her faith in God was and still is her hope for tomorrow.

Mrs. Rosie Ivery Pettygrue
My Favorite Teacher, Mentor, and Friend!

Thank you for everything you taught me and for encouraging me to be the best I could be. You are and have been a blessing to many children over the years.

Chapter 2

Defining Hope through Experiences

Have you ever felt useless and astounded by the way people have treated you or others? I experienced such moments in 1981. As a member of the women's choir, at my church in Ohio. Satan reared up his "ugly head" so often that people in the congregation could easily felt its effects. The "dark shadow" which cast over our group gave me a feeling of hopelessness and sadness. I felt as if I was standing at the top of Black Mountain in my home state of Kentucky, afraid and lonely.

"Why was I even here?" I often wondered. "How did something like this happen? I'm just a country girl who headed to Cleveland, Ohio, to better my life! I was seeking happiness in my marriage and in the church. I never expected Christian folk to act like this!" But, came to know that evilness can "pop up" from anywhere at any time.

I must admit that I was a bit naive and held the belief that church folks in the North were much nicer to one another than other places. For me, moving from the "Old South" meant moving away from a place where black men and women had historically been treated with a lot of disrespect. Unlike my new friend, who grew up in Cleveland and attended this church most of her life. I found myself in "foreign territory" consisting of "hot" and "cold" Christians.

Week after week, year after year, I continued on the journey with my "hot" and "cold" group members until one Sunday in 1999. That Sunday, I had made a choice to visit the church of a friend who had left our congregation. This young lady, I will call Sally. She invited me to attend a special program at her new place of worship. After the service, we stopped grab a bite to eat. During lunch, she ends up sharing why she left my church. The first thing she said was, "Let's talk about you for a minute." What about me?" I responded. "Have you heard something I am not aware of?"

"No, no." Sally replied. "I just want to know how you can stay there and be so unhappy.

"What makes you think I am unhappy?" I asked.

"Well, to begin." She said, "I am not the only one who feels that way. Many members have noticed the expressions on your face and the other ladies when you sing. It just looks like you don't belong with them. In other words, there is no *joy* on your face when you're standing up front singing with them. Personally, I don't think they like you," she went on to say.

"Wow!" I thought to myself. "Can you tell all of that by just looking at us?" I asked. After a brief moment of speechlessness, I shared a confession, "Okay Sally, let me be honest with you. I have never felt comfortable with the group. There has always been tension between myself and some of the members. It seems that a couple of them want to be 'more important' than others."

Sally asked, "Have you ever spoken up for yourself or asked them to meet about the discrepancies among the group?"

I assured her with a big, "Yes! But, certain people are best friends with the director and that's another story."

Sally thoughtfully reminded me, "It's not about their friendship, let's focus on you. You are the one being mistreated. No one deserves to be treated with such cruelty. Just remember, God is not just at Good Shepherd Baptist Church. He's everywhere. You are His child. He loves you and wouldn't want you to be unhappy while serving Him." Sally paused for a second then said, "Have you ever considered leaving the group or the church?"

Of course, I was uncomfortable and unhappy singing with a group who didn't want me in it or appreciate me as a person. Who wouldn't feel bad, always being left out of group outings or never asked for input? No one is perfect. I can't lead every song or attend every outing but did the best I could to meet group obligations. Flashbacks of antagonism, disrespect, jealousy, verbal, and physical abuse of my past were staring me in the face, once again. I had taught myself to humbly overlook things for so long that I did not realize I was accepting what was taking place. Yet, I reminded myself, certainly, people had treated me wrong and even made me sad but who had I done this same thing to?"

Before I received my salvation, and truly understood God's purpose for me, I reacted to things in a worldly manner. Nonetheless, I still can't recall a time that I had ever treated anyone as mean as the ladies in my choir group had treated me. During my conversation with Sally, I began to feel somewhat responsible for some of my own heartache. I started to understand how God places experiences in front of us to guide us. Just like, signs placed along roads to give us a choice of which way to go and help steer us in the right direction. Admittedly, I didn't always choose the right path during the mist of the storm with severe lightening threatening to strike.

As I reflect, a holiday performance comes to mind. Our choir group was invited to sing for a Christmas program at a local church. All group members committed to going. We even agreed upon the outfit and colors we'd wear. Signs of bitterness "showed up" regarding our performance. One of the members had purchased beautiful Christmas scarves for all of the women to wear around their necks, except me. Our location on the list allowed me to seek refuge in the ladies room where I sought to gather a red scarf or flower.

The conversation with Sally encouraged me to become more committed to living solely for Jesus. I had spent the last few years trying to please these people who gave me nothing but heartache and anguish. The things that took place illustrates why it is important to examine and know the Biblical meaning of hope. All I had to do was trust Jesus and be concerned about pleasing Him knowing that he'd see me through any and every challenge faced.

From Faith Comes Hope

Sometimes the most important questions remain dormant in the "shadows of our thoughts" but can crystalize in a single moment of time. The visit I had with Sally did just that for me. In one respect, her questions and comments brinked as being "nosey" and "condescending." Yet, her "sincere display of concern" allowed me to see that she acted out of love and concern for my best interests. "Why didn't He fix things when we first started off?"

Engrossed in feelings of hurt and disappointment, I had listened to Sally express her feelings about how I allowed myself to be treated. She had experienced disappointment in seeing Christians disrespect one another. As a Christian, she felt a certain sadness concerning such matters of faith. My thoughts kept returning to what God said about love in Matthew 22:37-39. The longer I contemplated them changing, the more I realized that these people really didn't understand what Christian love and unity meant. "Was it their fault how they treated me or my fault that I accepted it? Had I made a fatal error?"

Ever since my conversation with Sally, I have been looking closely at people "inside" and "outside" of the church setting. Observing, their response to disappointments. I even observed how often people expressed being disappointed in someone or something else. As life revolves, what do we really understand about loving others the way that He loves us?

One Sunday, a homosexual male walks into the church wanting to learn more about Jesus and being saved. He faithfully committed to going through all of the new member steps before he expressed a desire to serve. Some member's acknowledged that he was "a little flamboyant" and decided to avoid him as much as possible. He later shared with me during a one-on-one conversation that he wanted to live according to God's Word but felt unaccepted by people of the church.

Another Sunday, a young lady walked the doors of my church with her two young children. During altar call she asked for a special prayer where she confined that her husband had been abusive to her and the kids so she left Alabama for Georgia to get away from him. She found a job but expressed that living in a new city and not knowing anyone left her feeling lonely and depressed. Her concern was for emotional support and safety. She had been a Christian but lost faith in God because of the way negative church members responded to her in the past. Some of the ladies in our church reacted negatively to her also. Little did they know the only reason she visited with our church was because someone on the job had suggested it.

One day, a teenager called wishing to discuss a negative message posted about her on a social media page. She and her best friend eventually discovered that they liked the same boy. Her friend decided to post that her family had been homeless and had lived in a shelter for a while and that she'd been with several boys at school.

The teen was embarrassed and felt betrayed that information shared in confidence had become public knowledge at school and online for the whole world to see. She contemplated suicide. Can gossip be so emotionally damaging that it can have an individual ready to give up on life? What does God say about of hope in times of disappointment and despair?

Discontent from family, friends, and other relationships doesn't only come from dramatic situations like those mentioned. When God doesn't allow things to go our way, we may find ourselves disappointed. That's when doubt seeps in our spirit and all hope is lost because of our lack of faith in His promises. Have you ever found yourself in such a place before? I have, when offering to help a friend out during a stressful time in her life only to receive a negative message from her. The message stated I had "overstepped" my boundaries. My heart felt the sting of a thousand bees. I prayed over and over, "God please relieve me of this pain and help me move forward with being a good servant." No amount of singing my favorite songs or baking brownies for my grandchildren could remove the pain I felt in my heart.

I spent the next few weeks, reading and writing about things people had shared with me over the years regarding what helped them grow spiritually. I wondered what God thought about my plight regarding the matter. Would I be asked to change my scheduled plans to speak at an engagement where this person would be attending? Did God even care about what I was experiencing? Did he recall the amount of time and energy I had put into helping this person?

Like the young teen embarrassed over her past condition, I felt embarrassed and disappointed too. My offer to do what I thought was Christian service for someone in need began to feel "a little trivial" and "selfish of me." I failed to consider that this person had already made provisions although I wanted to help. It felt "a little stupid" to pray for someone's event to be successful. Satan tends to "stir up petty ways" of disappointing us when we're in the midst of "stirring up" our faith.

Sometimes I get excited and stay busy concentrating on doing things the way I believe they should be done. This unfortunately means I'm placing less focus on God's plans for me. When this happens, I'm less prepared for crisis management. When things go wrong, I am ready to blame God. Scripture says this about blame:

"Count it all joy, my brothers, when you meet trials of various kinds, for you know that the testing of your faith produces steadfastness. And let steadfastness have its full effect, that you may be perfect and complete, lacking in nothing" (James 1:2-4).

Confidence

As I thought deeply about myself and others, I wanted to reflect more on the topic of confidence. Many of us are lacking in this area. Often, we get confused about what it means to have confidence in God and being self-confident. Sometimes, we think because we are knowledgeable in an area that we're always right. God wants us to consider Him in all that we do. The Scripture tells us that, "The Lord taketh my part with them that help me: therefore shall I see my desire upon them that hate me. It is better to trust in the Lord than put confidence in man. It is better to trust in the Lord than to put confidence in princes" (Psalms 118:7-9).

As we go through life's journeys it's important to consider God's promises. Our confidence in God empowers us with energy to accomplish anything set before us. Fear, doubt, anxiety, and worry can be driven away with the assurance that God is near. Four verses in chapter four of the book of Philippians can help us see that we can find complete assurance in God. Philippians 4:5 tells us, "The Lord is near." Philippians 4:7 states, "And the peace of God will guard your hearts and your minds." Philippians 4:13 states, "I can do all things through Him who strengthens me." While, Philippians 4:19 states, "And my God will supply all your needs."

Though the walk of faith is not an easy one, these verses provide a guarantee that if we allow God to live in us, He will work in our lives for and through us to accomplish all that we hope to achieve. Sometimes, like most of the individuals just mentioned share one thing in common; that is having too little faith. Everyone falls down sometimes. We have to find the strength to get back up. God promises us a new beginning. He alone is the "Author and Finisher of our faith." It doesn't matter what you've done or what someone has done to you, you can always begin again. Don't ever give up. Exercise your faith in God and proudly stand on His promises.

Waiting Faithfull on God

If you have ever felt like God has forgotten about you, you're not alone. During the periods of "waiting for God" to respond to your needs it is easy to lose hope. However, we must remember that God does not work according to our plans. He sometimes defers our plans in order for us to learn the lesson of waiting. The book of Proverbs affirms, "Hope deferred makes the heart sick." Many times, I have wondered how God could put me on hold for so long while He goes around blessing other people. I'm sure someone can agree it makes the heart ache.

We must come to realize that God is the God of our salvation. Trusting in Him and waiting patiently for Him is necessary in expressing our faith in Him. King David waited patiently for many years for God to deliver him from his enemies which also included King Saul and his own son Absalom. "I waited patiently for the Lord; He turned to me and heard my cry" (Psalms 40:1). Waiting for God is essential in learning His ways.

> *"Show me your ways O Lord; teach me your paths. Guide me in*
> *your truth and teach me, for you are the God of my salvation.*
> *I wait for you all the daylong" (Psalms 27:11-14).*

Joshua was a servant to Moses for more than 40 years. Much of that time was spent in the desert waiting for an entire sinful generation to die off. Moses wasn't very kind, yet Joshua served faithfully. Even after defeating the Amalekites (Exodus 17) with a huge victory, nothing changed for Joshua. Yet, he chose to remain faithful.

When God called on Joshua, he was ready. His faithfulness had shaped him and prepared him for God's calling on his life. We must be prepared to wait on God. Serving faithfully in whatever role He places you in is His way of shaping you and transforming us for the position that has our name on. The question is, Are you willing to be second in command and wait faithfully for God to order the steps in your life?

Waiting on God gives Him a sovereign place in our lives. Waiting builds a relationship with God. It acknowledges that He is the complete source of our *joy* and *well-being*. "The Lord waits to be gracious to you so He will be exalted. He waits to show mercy for the Lord is a God of justice. How blessed are all those who wait for Him" (Isaiah 30:18).

Learning how to wait patiently for God's directions will assist us with our tendency to fret. Fretting is the very opposite of what God wants for us. He wants to give us *peace* and *joy*. By waiting on God and trusting in Him our physical as well as our spiritual health will be enhanced. Waiting on God helps us to develop peace, serenity, humility, meekness, and gentleness (Proverbs 3:8). Jesus said, "Blessed are the meek for they will inherit the earth" (Matthew 5:5).

Those who encounter trials should consider it joy. We must understand that trials are the testing of our faith which brings forth endurance. The Scripture advises us to allow patience and endurance to do a perfect work in our hearts (James 1:2-4). Through endurance our Christian character is developed and we grow spiritually. The Scripture also tells us to be anxious for nothing and to be thankful in all things (Philippians 4:6). God is in control of every aspect of our lives and that is enough to release the physical and psychological tensions that hold us captive (Psalms 31:15). As humans, we must stop trying to adjust things that we have no control of. God already said that there is a season for everything (Ecclesiastes 3:1-8).

Refuge in God

The book of Psalms mentions taking refuge in the Lord. The verses I observed say that those who take refuge in God are blessed. When we take refuge in God, He provides us with protection. Psalms 34:22 tells us that the Lord will save those who take shelter in Him. Christians often have an immediate need to seek shelter when life's storms are hurling down on them and violent winds are blowing our lives out of control. God is our protection and shelter from the storm.

Taking refuge doesn't only mean to take shelter when things are going wrong. His protection encompasses a wider span. The Lord wants us to come unto Him for the sake of our souls. In Matthew 11:28-30, He says, "Come to me, all you who are weary and burdened, and I will give you rest." God is telling us that His love for us is not limited to temporary protection but it is boundless.

Refuge in God means that we can look at the example in 2 Samuel, when David took shelter from the hand of his enemy Saul. He acknowledged that God was his protection when he realized that there was no other hiding place. The same stands for us. When going through a trial or feeling like the bottom has fallen out of our lives, remember Jesus is our refuge and the rock of our salvation. He can lead us through, around, and out of the storm when we ask Him to.

When Being Faithful is Painful

Sometimes, being faithful is challenging. God does require that we be religious or divine people, He wants us to be holy. The rest comes from Him. Being "churchy" and all "puffed up" on religion without having the right relationship with God is not what He wants. He wants us to die for Him. In other words, we must decrease so that He can increase in us. John 3:30 tells us that He must become greater and we must become less.

Change is painful but the Bible commands us to pray always so that our faith increases. Our faith grows increasingly (2 Thessalonians 1:3) by living on the promises of God. By receiving His word and living according to His commandments we receive additional faith from God. Romans tells us that "faith comes from hearing the message, and the message is heard through the word about Christ" (Romans 10:17, NIV).

Becoming more faithful requires us to stop thinking so highly of ourselves and think in accordance with the measure of faith God gives to us. I call these "growing pains." This type of growth tells us to move problems to the mountain from whence cometh our help. It also tells us to concentrate on trusting God and praising Him in all things. I know it is hard to trust God when you can't see anything going your way lately. This is the time you can cultivate your faith by giving God the opportunity to reveal Himself. You are His child and you will know His voice. The Bible says this is when you will prosper.

Waiting

One area of our lives where we often lack is having enough patience and faith to wait for our blessings. The Lord controls the "traffic lights" of our lives. The answer is "go" when He wills it so. Many of us already know that God has a particular time and purpose for everything concerning us. But, we still get anxious, excited, and ready to have things our way, and in our time. Just as a plane can't take off until its passenger boards, the doors close, everyone is safely strapped in, and the pilot has been given the okay for take-off, we must learn to wait on Him. God's time is not our time. His timing is a "road map" of life that can guide our way.

We don't like to wait but we must. Moses had to wait when he was called to deliver the children out of Israel. He served his father-in-law Jethro 40 years before God allowed Him to be released (Exodus 2:21). Abraham had to wait on God to receive what was promised to him (Hebrew 6:15). God promised Abraham and Sarah a child in their old age. They grew impatient. As a result, Sarah gave Abraham her servant Hagar who bore a son called Ishmael. Thirteen years later, He delivered on His promise and gave Abraham and Sarah their son, Isaac (Genesis 21). God heard the faithful prayers of Zechariah and his wife Elizabeth who was barren. God heard their prayer while they remained faithful and blessed them with fruitfulness. A son was given to them by the name of John who we refer to as John the Baptist (Luke 1-3). Joseph is another example of an individual who remained faithful to God. Held, three years in prison for doing the right thing; He loved and honored God even during hardship by remaining faithful and patient. As days became years, God moved Joseph from the prison to the palace (Genesis 37-41).

Many of us cannot identify with every situation mentioned in the Scriptures but we can identify with Hababbuk the minor prophet who "grew impatient" waiting for God to answer his request (Hababbuk 1:2). Like Hababbuk, we may grow impatient in waiting for God to answer our requests. Hebrews 10:36 says, "For you have need of patience, that, after you have done the will of God, you might receive the promise." Most certainly, the need exists to grow in this area of patience. Patience does not come easy, but with God's help we can get there.

Most of us are impatient about something or the other. We must change our perspective on how we react to things. We have to come to understand that nobody is perfect and that illness, stress, and hardships can often cloud the one's ability to reason. In knowing this, may we take our minds off of ourselves to pray for others while God keeps working things out on our behalf.

Waiting on the Lord and keeping His way can be challenging when facing wickedness and strife. However, you must not give up on praying and trusting in Him. God told parables to his disciples to show them that they should always pray and never give up (Luke 18:1-8). Sometimes, we pray hard and long for situations in our lives yet nothing seems to happen. We begin to believe, God has forgotten about us and our prayers will go unanswered. But, God is concerned about us. He is working on our behalf even when we are in doubt. The Scriptures advise us to, "Wait for the Lord; be strong, and let your heart take courage. Yes, wait for the Lord" (Psalms 27:14).

Trust

Many years of my youth, I spent time wondering if God loved me and He heard my prayers. I was saddened by the turmoil in my childhood. I spent much of my time devising ways to make myself happy. I had been introduced to God at an early age. However, I spent a lot of time trying to fix circumstances I had absolutely no control of. The gloom and unhappiness in my life seemed never ending. Fortunately for me, my grandfather told me about trusting in God. I learned how to faithfully trust Him and my life was transformed.

What Trusting in God Means

Trusting in God is defined by believing in His love for us, believing He knows and wants what is best for our lives, and He has the power to help us through any situation. Often Christians, known as believers, can act very much like unbelievers. We place our trust in the stock market, lottery, banks, casinos, friends, and even the government. Somehow, God and His word lands last on our list.

We can do nothing apart from Jesus. He said, "I am the vine; you are the branches. If you remain in me and I in you, you will bear much fruit; apart from me you can do nothing" (John 15:15, NIV). We need Him for everything we do. Sadly, many people believe they are in control of their own lives and try to fix things themselves. The results are usually unsuccessful because they block God's help. God wants to be first in our lives. He wants us to trust Him and put our full confidence in Him for everything.

Not My Will, But Thy Will Lord

I tried trusting myself and other people for many years and ended up hurting worse than I started out. This taught me not to believe in man. If you want something done right the first time, you have to go to God. If you don't want people to have control of your circumstances, you must leave them out of "your business" while you take care of His business. Don't even try to fix the matter yourself, turn it over to God. Trust in Him for He knows what is best for you.

One of the greatest blessings of having faith in God and gaining salvation is having His spirit live within you. He knows the beginning, middle, and end of everyone's life story. "Trust in the Lord with all your heart and lean not on your own understanding; in all your ways submit to Him, and He will make your paths straight" (Proverbs 3:5-6, NIV). When things start coming your way, know that it is God's grace working in your favor.

Grace through Faith in God

Experience teaches us that we are incapable of saving ourselves from sin and that none of us are righteous. The Scripture tells us, "There is none righteous, no not one" (Romans 3:10). However, Paul tells us that by grace we are saved through faith; not that of ourselves, but it is a gift of God" (Ephesians 2:8). Grace is a gift from God which is part of our salvation. Faith is our acceptance and trust in God's grace.

The grace God has for us springs from His love for us (1 John 4:8). God sent His son to save us (John 3:16) this is when He sent grace. Acts 20:24, tells us the conditions of salvation and grace. Every person living has the opportunity to receive grace. God is willing to save us but He has determined that we have a part to play. The Scripture tells us that "God presented Christ as a sacrifice of atonement, through the shedding of his blood – to be received by faith…" (Romans 3:25, NIV).

Paul had a message for the Ephesian Christians about salvation of grace through faith. Paul's message also relates to us today. By doing as the Ephesians, we also will be saved by grace through faith in God. By making a faithful effort to be obedient and please God, we can be assured that He will make all grace abound according to His will for us.

An Examination of Faith

Churches are overflowing with people who think they belong to God; however, they are sadly mistaken. God knows every true believer

(2 Timothy 2:19). Paul wrote, you must "Examine yourselves to see whether you are in the faith; test yourselves." Do you not realize that Christ Jesus is in you – unless, of course, you fail the test?" (2 Corinthians 13:5, NIV).

Constant Hope

At times, the journey called life may make you feel as if you're walking through a maze or a museum. In the maze, you may discover that you are constantly thinking and using strategies to find your way out. In the museum, you may find that you are too busy admiring the beauty, techniques, and the significance of great works of art. Perhaps, hope can be thought of in the same way. David, Abraham, Jeremiah, and Job did not have the aid of electronics and other technical devices to keep them connected. They stayed connected by relying on prayer and talking to God as much as they could. They had persistent hope in God. Persistent hope worked back then and can also today. Hope requires being patient in tribulation and constant in prayer. Constant doesn't mean every minute, it means persevere in prayer. Don't stop, be devoted, and make prayer a habit. God deserves more than an accidental pocket call. He loves us, He wants to help us and He deserves our praise.

Waiting for the Right Answer

A dear friend, Denise was a Christian woman who faithfully committed to serving God. She has worked hard to complete her education and advance in her profession. But, the main hope and focus for Denise was to find herself the "right mate." After several years of waiting and experiencing flopped dates, she was nearly convinced that the "Mr. Right" may not exist for her. However, a visit to her hometown for a class reunion reunited with her childhood sweetheart. Great! However, another obstacle stood in the way. He was in the middle of a divorce. After many months of waiting, they decided to start dating. Normally, she would have lost hope. But, she waited this time. The two dated successfully for almost a year. During this time, she discovered something else about the relationship. She discovered her relationship with God was much more important than the one she had with her childhood sweetheart. She called it quits. She decided to "wait patiently" for God to bless her with the person He has for her.

Faith for Healing

Ralph a devout deacon of one of the churches I attended was always concerned that his wife Georgia had no interest in Christianity, church, or spiritual things. A professed atheist, she refused to thank God or pray for anybody or anything. For many years, her shield of defense stood its ground. Yet, Ralph never gave up on his hope that she would one day accept Christ as her personal Savior.

Finally, after many years and still clinging to his hope, Ralph received news that Georgia had passed out at work and would be hospitalized. Upon his arrival to the hospital, the doctor informed him that she had mass on her brain and her condition seemed hopeless. I remember Ralph stepping out of the room and asking the nurse where the chapel was. He asked me to join him. Ralph's faith and trust in God was rewarded with a message from the doctor saying "I believe we can fix the problem," she has just responded positively to the medication."

After her hospital stay Georgia gained a different outlook on life. She began visiting a church on the east side of Cleveland. She became a member over 30 years ago and to this day is a faithful worker at the church. Ralph has since passed away. Surely, he left this earth with the *joy* in his heart of knowing that his faith in God healed and saved his precious wife.

Chapter 3

Unrighteous Frustration: A Refusal to Wait on God

Frustration can well up and touch our lives like a tornado with strong winds. It can wreak havoc all around. Besides the damage caused to everything in its path, the powerful downdrafts and updrafts leave a strong rotation on turbulent thunderstorms.

Frustration is our response to being unfulfilled. It intensifies with the degree of the storm. Though "the condition" may be temporary it draws forth an extreme reaction. Accompanied by unresolved problems, feelings of dissatisfaction, and is often accompanied by anxiety and depression. Many times hope is blocked by disappointment and anger.

What Causes Frustration?

Interference with Satisfaction

Frustration is something everyone experiences at one time or another. It's that burning feeling in the pit of your stomach when something doesn't go the way you want or expect it to. *Merriam-Webster* defines frustration as a deep sustained sense of logic or a state of uncertainty and dissatisfaction commonly caused by external factors. By identifying the causes of your frustration you will become better equipped to avoid some of its affects – anger, fear, hatred, and other negative emotions. Frustration can be caused by external factors or internal factors.

An example of an external factor would be heading to an important job interview and half way there realizing that your portfolio was still on the sofa. You have one hour to get to the interview and believe you have enough time to turn around and grab it. You're able to retrieve it but traffic is a nightmare once on the road again. Traffic is creeping along extremely slow. Finally, traffic gets moving again and your destination is in view. But, you can't quite reach it yet because you are unable to find a parking space nearby. You ended up parking a block away; and you are nearly breathless from running to your destination. With just three minutes left at arrival, you think, "Wow, I made it." You arrive breathless to the reception desk and become totally frustrated when the receptionist shares that the interview was cancelled and the position has been filled.

At first, you blame yourself for leaving the portfolio and running so close to the deadline, thinking, "Maybe I should have hit the road a little earlier." Anger and disappointment in yourself, the situation that caused the traffic jam, and lack of parking spaces didn't allow you to accomplish what you had set out to do.

A feeling of helplessness may set in, after spending precious time planning and preparing for something. Only to realize, what you wanted so badly to happen had been blocked. The very thing, hoped to bring satisfaction just delivered a powerful blow of distress. We become distressed when we have to wait for something or when something doesn't happen as planned or expected. The pain of dissatisfaction forces us to choose whether we wait on God or depend on man to bring us joy.

Internal frustration takes place when an individual has competing goals. For instance you want to give your family the best way of living that you possibly can – a nice home, food, shelter, nice clothes, good schools, and everything else that goes with the "good life."

An example of an internal factor is the inability to accomplish a goal or act on an emotion because of an actual or fictitious discrepancy. For instance, your son is a "star quarterback" at his high school playoff game and college scouts will recruit players for teams that night. But, you already made the commitment of working overtime that day. In this case, internal frustration exists because you want to provide the best for your child and also be there to support them. However, it is impossible for you to be in two places at the same time; unlike Him.

Unwarranted Attack

We long for satisfaction of our needs and desires. But, may fail to realize that the fulfillment of our needs and desires are not in the hands of those we look to. So, we become frustrated when others do not conform to our expectations. Leading to justification of the reasons for the resentment we may feel toward others.

Suppose, you go out on a hot summer day to the ice cream parlor to enjoy your favorite flavor of ice cream. But, the person in front of you just purchased the last scoop. You become transitorily frustrated because something that you wanted to satisfy your desire didn't occur —enjoyment of that specific-brand of black walnut ice cream from this particular parlor because the person in front of you blocked your wish.

On the other hand, if the ice-cream parlor has "a secret stash" of your favorite flavor in the back, you can still enjoy what you wanted and the frustration will fade away. However, if the person in front of you got the "actual last scoop" your satisfaction is threatened. You will likely become annoyed and grow more uncomfortable as you wait with anticipation. When the clerk asks you to "step to the side to wait" and calls another customer to the counter you become more anxious. "Will I have to wait for nothing? Why couldn't he or she go back to check now and make the other customer wait? After all, I was here first – it all seems, so unfair.

True attacks on our emotions always involve some form of unfairness and are in violation of God's plan for our lives. We should feel angry by "acts of destruction to God's creation" such as the intentional setting of forest fires or killing animals for wealth and crimes against others. Especially when an injustice is done to a child or a helpless human being. The anger expressed in most situations has nothing to do with God's "redemptive purpose" of destroying the bad to enhance the good. God designed anger and blessed it to destroy sin. But, unrighteous anger condemns anyone who opposes His purpose, "because human anger does not produce the righteousness that God desires" (James 1:20, NIV).

Paul implies in Ephesians that not all anger is sin. He presumes that we can be angry without being ruled by sin. This would have to be accomplished by distinguishing between "righteous" and "unrighteous" anger. Paul tells us, "In your anger do not sin" (Ephesians 4:26). This chapter discusses unrighteous anger and characteristics of God reflected in righteous anger.

Unrighteous Anger

Unrighteous anger flows from pride, selfishness, fear, anxiety, jealousy, and self-centeredness. An example of unrighteous anger can be seen in the life of King Saul. Saul became very angry when the people of Israel publicly praise David for his military conquest. Saul became jealous because David was being credited with accomplishing much more than he (1 Samuel 18: 8-9). Saul's anger stemmed from pride, jealousy, and self-preservation.

Using Unrighteous Anger to Suppress Choice

An example of this is often seen in the church kitchen. The head cook, Gina, who normally prepares the meals and has helpers peeling potatoes and washing vegetables. The church event planner, Porsha, enters the kitchen and in a loud voice of authority started telling the cook how she would have done things. The helpers quickly scurry from the prep area.

Gina was caught in the middle of her task and could not leave her spot. The event planner had a mean attitude and snapped. "I can't believe this is all you have done!" Porsha scolded her in a sarcastic voice. "Don't you know how to prepare for large groups, and why is it taking so long to get started?"

Gina refrained from making direct contact with the event planner. "Yes I do," Gina replied in a low mumble. "My staff and I would like to finish what we are doing." The staff returned, finished their work and everyone hurried to another area to escape the event planner.

What prompted Porsha's attack? It wasn't the most vicious, but it set an "uncomfortable tone" for the rest of the day. Perhaps, Gina was trying to make a point and show her authority. If the other women had choices, Porsha might have been left feeling ashamed, empty, lonely, or vulnerable. Her goal in this event may have been self-preservation.

Righteous anger differs in that it does not suppress choice. Righteous anger offers pain only to induce transformation.

Unrighteous Anger as Heart Management

The root of anger is in the heart of man. The Scripture helps us to understand that the heart of a person is actually the source of his actions and words. In Proverbs 4:23, we read that the heart is the wellspring of life. In Luke 6:43-45, Jesus explains the heart principle: "No good tree bears bad fruit nor does a bad tree bear good fruit. Each tree is recognized by its own fruit…" The root of the tree represents the heart of man. Jesus is making the point that actions and words flow out of the heart of man. Therefore, righteous anger is rooted in God and is focused on doing God's Will for His glory. Unrighteous anger is rooted in self-centeredness and is focused on self-glory.

Unrighteous anger is not only rooted in the heart of man, but it seeks to occupy the empty spaces of our lives through "spirit possession." It is rage that makes us attack others over anything we claim ownership to and believe is essential to our well-being. Our hearts are speaking, "It's mine!" To possess others by planning, plotting, and scheming against them becomes the lifelong goal of many people. In Isaiah 8:21, such actions are referred to as rage.

Unrighteous anger condemns any person standing in its way. Righteous anger desires only to bless our lives. Unrighteous anger suppresses choice and fuels hatred and pain while the wounds of righteous anger are inflicted only as a warning with the intention of blessing. The essence of unrighteous anger is hatred and the love of sin. "Unrighteous anger" is filled with rage, control, and violation of God's Word. However the essence of "righteous anger" is hatred of sin and love of God righteousness.

When we rage against others for the pain and suffering they inflict upon us, we rage against God. Unrighteous anger separates us from God and delivers Satan's desires. It leaves us naked and defenseless. We must learn how to go to God and repent for our unrighteous. It is written in 1 John 1:9, "If we confess our sins, He is faithful and just and will forgive us our sins and purify us from all unrighteousness." We must seek God's Word for guidance and wisdom to manage our anger in all situations.

Righteous Anger

Righteous anger flows from experiences of injustice, jealousy, being sinned against, or when someone chooses to mock God. Jesus displayed righteous anger when he chased the money changers out of the temple (John 2:12-16). The money changers were mocking God by turning His house into a den of thieves. Jesus' anger flowed from "righteous anger" out of His respect for the House of God, God's character, and integrity.

An example of this happening to you would be someone accusing you of doing something wrong and you character gets publicly smeared and thrown in the media and other sources of communication. You would have the right to experience the God-given emotion of anger because you were innocent and sinned against by others due to slander.

"Righteous anger" is not self-justifying or malicious. Instead, it's instilled with the sadness and gloom that is rich in desire and hope. This type of anger advises, invites, and wounds only for the greater transformation and redemption of man. It allows the defense to be seen as an issue between the offender and God.

Ephesians 4:26-27 tells us to, "Be angry, and yet not sin; do not let the sun go down on your anger, and do not give the devil an opportunity." We know that some place in the Bible anger and jealousy are attributed to God, therefore we know that not all anger or jealousy is evil. In Ephesians 4:27-28, the text reveals righteous anger and how we can express anger in a way that brings glory to God.

The Bible teaches in Ephesians 4:26-27, 31-32, to let bitterness and wrath and anger and slander be put away from you, along with all malice. Ephesians 4:26 and 31, seems conflicting; however, it refers to two types of anger. The one which expresses self-manifestation (the flesh) is to be" put off" and the one that's a manifestation of God's righteousness are to be "put on."

Righteous Anger and Willingness to Wait On God

The initial reaction of anger to anything that happens to us may be righteous or unrighteous. It is impossible to distinguish between the righteous anger and the unrighteous anger because emotions are so involved. The arousal of anger creates questions and your righteous anger becomes distressed and struggles with God: Why are you letting this happen to me? When is it going to stop? What are you trying to teach me about myself?

The Bible gives us an example in Psalms 77:6-9, of how the psalmist became confused and angry over waiting for God to answer him. His focus moved from hurt and anger to pondering over the disposition of God. The apostle James described man's frustration:

> "You desire but do not have, so you kill. You covet but you cannot get what you want, so you quarrel and fight. You do not have because you do not ask God.
>
> When you ask, you do not receive, because you ask with wrong motives, that you may spend what you get on your pleasures" (James 4:2-3).

When our desires go unfulfilled we can become vicious. The only way to avoid such actions is by surrendering to God. He is the only one who can satisfy our needs and desires. He does this by His own authority. He makes us wait, intensifying our desires. By taking complete control away from us, He compels us to trust more. Or, not trust in Him if we so choose.

Unrighteous anger trusts in the "power of self" and refusal to trust in God. The Bible connects hope to God and a willingness to wait for Him. "We wait and in hope for the Lord; he is our help and our shield" (Psalms 33:20). And, "I wait for the Lord, my soul waits, and in his word I put my hope" (Psalms 130:5).

Waiting is having the assurance that God will bring justice in our behalf. He will satisfy our deepest desires, but everything happens in His time and not ours. While you wait and learn to trust Him completely, your heart will struggle with righteous anger for answers that only God can provide.

The Glory of Righteous Anger

Our emotions are tarnished by emblems of God. Our ugliest motions poorly reflect His glory and dishonors humanity. Our emotions are like a distorted negative which reflects the image in reverse of its true color. God who is light is reflected in darkness instead of in His glory and honor and we who are in darkness reflect ourselves as light.

It is important to know and understand God's character. God's character gives us discernment to know who is from God and who is not from God. God's character is represented by all of the following:

Justice and Righteousness

God's character is justice because He will always make wrongs right. Justice is a term used for right. Justice and righteousness are used synonymously in the Bible. Because God is holy, He is righteous. His righteousness and holiness in dealing with mankind is declared throughout the Scriptures. We must understand sin in order to understand God's righteousness. Sin represents lawlessness (1John 3:4) and iniquity (Daniel 9:4-5; Micah 2:1; James 3:6). God provides His righteousness as a gift to sinners who accept His son as their savior based on His grace and mercy in response to our faith (Romans 3:23-26; Ephesians 2:3-7).

Goodness

God is originally good; the essence of God is good. "The goodness of God endureth continually" (Psalms 52:1). His character is goodness because He is good all the time. Psalms 34:8 shares, "Taste and see that the Lord is good; blessed is the man who takes refuge in Him" (NIV). The goodness of God is seen in God's decrees, in His creation, His laws, and His providences. It is written in the Scripture, "And God saw everything He had made, and behold, it was very good" (Genesis 1:31).

Holy

And God is holy. Holy in the Greek language means righteous. God is never wrong, He is always right. "There is none holy like the Lord; there is none besides you; there is no rock like our God" (1 Samuel 2:2). We are told in 1 John 1:7, that if we walk in the light we will fellowship with God because He is in the light, and Jesus' blood will cleanse us from all of our sins.

Because God is spirit (John 4:24), He is omniscient, omnipotent, and omnipresent. God was there in the beginning (Genesis 1:1) which means He always was and always will be (Revelation 1:8).

Omniscient

God knows everything. The Bible attest to God's all-knowing power in Isaiah 40:28; Job 37:16; Psalm 147:5; 1 John 3:20; Romans 11:33 and many Scriptures. "Omniscient" is defined in *The Random House Unabridged Dictionary* (2006) as "having complete knowledge, awareness, or understanding; perceiving all things." The Bible explains that nothing is hidden from God's knowledge. Paul stated, "There is no creature hidden from God's sight, but all things are naked and open to the eyes of Him to whom we must give account" (Hebrews 4:13).

Omnipotent

God is not limited by what He can do. The Greek word translated as "Omnipotent" is *pantokrator*, meaning "All-ruling" or "Almighty." The Scriptures tell us that God has all authority to do as He pleases (Isaiah 46:10-11), and to see the fulfillment of His plans. Jesus tells us that "with God all things are possible" (Matthew 19:26).

Omnipresent

God is present in all places at all times. God is present in Heaven, on His throne, and in every place at the same time. "Omnipresent" means to be everywhere, at the same time. The only way to explain this is to consider that God had a body and shape like ours. Genesis 1:26 stated that He made man in His own image. David answers the question of how God can be everywhere in Psalms 139:7 when God asked, "Where can I go from your Spirit?"

Immutable

Throughout the Bible, a myriad of verses teach us about the immutability of God. Numbers 23:19 affirms, "God is not a man, that He should lie, nor a son of man, that He should change His mind.

Does He speak and then not act? Does He promise and not fulfill?" His immutability is further affirmed in Malachi 3:6 where God asserts, "I the Lord do not change." In Numbers 23:19, 1 Samuel 15:29; Isaiah 46:9-11; Ezekiel 24:14 and James 1:17, we are told, "Every good and perfect gift is from above and comes down from the Father of lights, with whom is no variableness nor shadow of turning."

The sun is the shadow which Bible refers to. The sun eclipse, turns, and casts its shadow over the entire earth. As it turns, it appears and disappears. In one location it may be day while in another it is night. However, because God is the light, there is no darkness or change. He is unchangeable. God is holy and cannot turn into darkness because every good and perfect gift is in Him and comes from Him. Hebrews 13:8 said that "Jesus Christ is the same yesterday and today, and forever."

Sovereign

Sovereignty means that God, as the creator and ruler of the universe, has complete authority and control over His creation. Further, he has the right to do whatever He chooses. The sovereignty of God is supported numerous places in the Bible. In Psalm 115:3, the psalmist affirms that "God is in heaven; he does whatever pleases him" (NIV). We are nothing to Him, but because he loves all that He has created and makes provisions for us.

Nonbelievers would see God's sovereignty as "a stumbling block" because He demands total control. They fear that He will interfere with or eliminate all of the evil they strive to inflict upon the people of the world. Even though we cannot comprehend why God allows evil, we are called to be faithful and trust in His goodness toward us. We are instructed in Ecclesiastes 7:13-14, "Consider the work of God: Who can make straight what he has made crooked? In the day of prosperity be joyful, and in the day of adversity consider: God has made the one as well as the other, so that man may not find out anything that will be after him" (ESV).

Love

The Bible tells us that God is love. According to 1 John 4:8, "Whoever does not love does not know God, because God is love. God's love is discussed throughout Chapter Four of 1 John, which encourages us to trust only God. Also, to test the spirits to know whether or not they are of God. It also, lets us know that we belong to Him. And, gives us instructions for living Godly lives.

In 1 Corinthians 12:3, we learn that deception takes place in the spiritual arena aimed at convincing us that God is not who He says He is. False prophets belong to the Devil and aim to destroy everything belonging to Him. The love we share with one another testifies to the nature of God. It confirms His presence in our lives. Our faith is a testimony of our trust and belief in God's love for us. The love God has for us and His assurance of eternal life makes me believe as Paul when he stated:

> *"For I am persuaded that neither death nor life, nor angels nor principalities nor powers, nor things present nor things to come, nor height nor depth, nor any other created thing, shall be able to separate us from the love of God which is in Christ Jesus our Lord" (Romans 8:38-39).*

Merciful

One way of explaining God's mercy is to simply tell you that God loves us so much that He sacrificed Himself for our sins. He is compassionate and forgiving to people even when they do not deserve it. Instead of giving us the punishment we deserve; He offers us a way for salvation. God's mercy is an act of compassion for an offense which normally would be punished.

The prophet Daniel declares, "To the Lord belong mercies and forgiveness, though we have rebelled against him" (Daniel 9:9). But, even though we deserve His harsh judgment God pardons us. Jeremiah expresses in Lamentations 3:22, "His compassions fail not."

Trinity

The Bible emphasizes that there is one God. However, we know from reading the Bible that God manifest Himself in three distinct persons: God the Father, God the Son (Jesus) and God the Holy Spirit. Unlike man, who lives in a three-dimensional world, God lives in a limitless, dimensional universe.

Unlike us, who can have individuals that look and act like us, God cannot be duplicated. He is spirit and can be different from the Son and the Holy Spirit. Yet the same as the Son and the Holy Spirit. In Genesis 1:26, during the creation of man, God said, "Let us make man in our image…" He also affirms in Isaiah 45:5, "I am the Lord, and there is no other, Besides Me there is no God." In John 10:30 Jesus spoke saying, "I and the Father are one."

The Triune God and Our Behavior

Believing in God's very existence has effects on man's behavior. Sadly, our unrighteous irritation, frustration, anger, and rage are sometimes how we reflect God. God exist for us as God the Father; however it is impossible to know God the Father without knowing God the Son. Jesus confirms the trinity when He spoke in John 15:26 saying, "When the Advocate comes, whom I will send to you from the Father, the Spirit of truth who comes from the Father, he will testify on my behalf. And Paul when speaking to the people of the Corinthian church exhorted: "Awake to righteousness and sin not: for some have no knowledge of God" (1 Corinthians 15:34 RV).

God's intention through our anger is to reflect what His intentions are for us. Darkness inverted becomes light. God loves us so much that even our unrighteous desires we reflect a legitimate plea to destroy an enemy. Throughout the Psalms, pleas are made demanding that evil ones suffer.

My hope for today is that your anger becomes more righteous and that you are more conformed to God's anger. By joining God's anger you are joining a holy purpose: to dismantle sin. The connection between God's anger to the fears of man is explained by the psalmist:

We are consumed by your anger
and terrified by your indignation.
You have set our iniquities before you,
our secret sins in the light of your presence.
All our days pass away under your wrath;
we finish our years with a moan.
The length of our days is 70 years—
or 80, if we have the strength;

yet their span is but trouble and sorrow,
for they quickly pass and we fly away.
Who knows the power of your anger?
For your wrath is as great as the fear that is due you.
Teach us to number our days aright,
that we may gain a heart of wisdom.
(Psalms 90:7-12, NIV)

Many Christians regard God's wrath as something they need to apologize for. However, God's wrath is appropriate for the fear that is due Him. While, some people may consider the wrath of God a fault in His character, others would rather not think about it at all. But, if we refuse to bow to Him, we will face His wrath disassembling the assumption of our impartiality. The psalmist asserts in Psalms 60:1-3 that God's anger is powerful and His wrath can cause the earth to tremble and man to stagger. God's anger removes our independence and forces us to acknowledge Him.

The wrath of God is an attribute which without He would be less than God. His wrath is His detestation of unrighteousness. The most incredible fact about it is that much of God's wrath has not been directed at mankind but at Himself. Though God made everything, His anger against sin is that it represents a wrong to His uninfringeable sovereignty. God the Father's wrath was even turned against His Son for a moment causing a splinter in the Trinity. God's wrath is mentioned over 600 times in the Old Testament and in the New Testament by 20 different words. Paul stated in Romans, "But, God demonstrates his own love for us in this: While we were still sinners, Christ died for us" (5:8, NIV).

Transformation from Unrighteous Anger

Even though there seems to be many barriers and stumbling blocks in the mist of our lives, there is hope. God is always ready to rescue us from the hands of the wicked. He may appear to pull back at times when we think we need Him most, but remember; He knows just what we need and when we need it. The psalmist tells us, "Be still before the Lord and wait patiently for Him; do not fret when men succeed in their ways, when they carry out their wicked schemes. Refrain from angry and turn from wrath; do not fret-it leads to evil" (Psalms 37:7-8).

Most of the battles we attempt to fight on our own only draw us into retaliating against something we have no control of and are not worth the time. Trying to solve it ourselves gets in the way of God doing what He does in our behalf. God requires us to wait to receive His grace and goodness. To be still and wait on the Lord avoids us falling into the wrath of God for not trusting Him. "Wait on the LORD: be of good courage, and he shall strengthen thine heart: wait, I say, on the Lord" (Psalm 27:14, KJV).

The Accomplishments of Righteous Anger

I am sure by now; you are wondering what righteous anger looks like in comparison to unrighteous anger and exactly what righteous anger can do for you. Let me begin by saying there is hope after despair. Whatever you are feeling against the person or persons you have fury against let it go. Ponder on the fact that your fury is only a tiny speck compared to the fury God had when He showed His wrath against His son rather than against us. Our anger is small in comparison. Again I remind you, His anger was for a define purpose, "His love for us." In righteous anger we join God in His anger against sin.

Righteous anger cautions, commands change, and wounds. I grew up believing that anger was something that only evil people have. As an abused child, I didn't realize the guilt I felt about the beatings I received were misdirected. Instead, I punished myself by trying to replace the pain with "superficial joy" and acting out in other behaviors. Solutions to my problems came after I became an adult and learned what God's Word says about anger. I was angry and too young to understand, but God was angry about what was happening to me. You too, have the opportunity to learn about God and partner with Him to grow.

The writer of Proverbs associated anger to foolishness; "Fools quickly show that they are upset, but the wise ignore insults" (Proverbs 12:16, NCV). And the apostle Paul encourages us to let our heavenly Father fight our battles: "My friends do not try to punish others when they wrong you, but wait for God to punish them with his anger. It is written: I will punish those who do wrong; I will repay them,' says the Lord" (Romans 12:19, NCV).

Christian counseling taught me how to express my feelings righteously! I am gratefully thankful for God's Word which set constraints and conditions for anger. God's Word lets us know no matter how upset we become, we are not justified to sin. "When you are angry, do not sin, and be sure to stop being angry before the end of the day" (Ephesians 4:26, NCV). I have found it very important to evaluate my role in conflicts as closely as possible to avoid as many negative interactions as possible. The book of James tells us to "Let every person be quick to hear, slow to speak, slow to anger; for the anger of man does not produce the righteousness of God" (James 1:19–20, ESV).

Righteous anger provides a warning to danger that is ahead. It informs you that you are in danger, and that something you may do or say could bring harm to yourself or others. Righteous anger informs the offender that something has happened that aims to destroy the relationship between the offender and God. We are appropriate in getting upset over sin but after the offense, we as Christians have the responsibility to take action against hatred, and oppression.

Those who indulge in unrighteous anger refuse to take the responsibility of bearing the pain and grief for the freedom of others. Instead they suppress freedom to fulfill their own selfish and empty emotions. Righteous anger however, never suppresses choice and it reveals any potential threat. It is our God given privilege to draw attention to the potential harm but to people with the choice of deciding what is right or wrong.

Anger The Motivation for Change

Anger is imperative for change because it reveals truths about the offender beliefs, values, sense of righteousness, and needs. Anger also presents opportunity for an individual to focus on constructive steps in moving forward spiritually and emotionally. A person must first analyze and understand where the anger is coming from. For example, the results may be related to feeling hurt and sadness due to loss, shame, humiliation, hatred, or fear. An individual may have a neurological reason for being hostile or violent. The change will come when we believe in the power of redemption. Our hearts may occasionally battle with the memories of sorrow, sadness, and confusion. Yet, our hearts will be strangely and abundantly blessed with the joy God gives us after blessing the offender with forgiveness.

Paying the price of redemption is for someone who has offended you. It is a hard and challenging experience. In the book, *Cry of the Soul*, writers Allender and Longman (1994) stated, "It is easier to feel no anger. But, the absence of anger is the choice to remain unaffected by sin." (p. 76). The writers proposed that righteous anger is needed when God's glory is violated.

Our unrighteous anger must be transformed into righteous anger as we learn to hate sin and love righteousness. In McCosh's book, *Motive Powers*, he noted that "We may be angry and sin not; but this disposition may become sinful, and this in the highest degree. It is so when it is excessive, when it is rage, and makes us lose control of ourselves. It is so, and may become a vice, when it leads us to wish evil to those who have offended us. It is resentment when it prompts us to meet and repay evil by evil. It is vengeance when it impels us to crush those who have injured us. It is vindictiveness when it is seeking out ingeniously and laboriously means and instruments to give pain to those who have thwarted us. Already sin has entered."

The process of transforming the emotional energy called anger from the unrighteous form to the righteous form requires that we: (1) Recognize the injustices, corruptions, and cruelty in the world for what they are – sin. (2) Use that anger as motivating energy instead of a allowing a destructive force control our destiny.

In the story of David and Goliath, we learn that Goliath, aggravated, teased, intimidated, and verbally abused his way into power over the Israelite army. David entered the Israelite camp to find a crippled and terrified army. When David was when disrespected by Goliath he did not become intimidated. Instead David who was overwhelmed with anger went to Saul and said, "The LORD who rescued me from the paw of the lion and the paw of the bear will rescue me from the hand of this Philistine..." (1 Samuel 17: 37, NIV). In David you can see righteous indignation at work. Just as David used the motivator or faith and obedience to defeat Goliath, you can use your faith in God to defeat any enemy.

Chapter 4

From Stress to Success

After giving an account of what sin, frustration, and anger does in the earlier chapters, I decided to share with you a couple of stories where people were experiencing stressful situations but the end result for having faith in God was success. The story of Rachel and Jacob ends in success as well as the story of Job.

One of the toughest experiences in life is waiting for something. Why do I have to wait so long for things to happen in our favor? Why does a man or woman have to wait for a good mate when he or she believes it's time? How long must I go through the heartache and anguish before he or she changes? How long do I trust God for a job or promotion? It is stressful to wait for something when you believe it is time for you to have it. Like Rachel faced stress in her life, so will some of us.

Jacob and Rachel: Faith in Love

Jacob found love at first sight. The moment he gazed upon Rachel, Jacob knew she was the one. Jacob knew he had found his true love in Rachel the daughter of Laban. When Jacob saw Rachel approaching the well where he was watering his sheep, "he went over and rolled the stone away from the mouth of the well and watered his uncle's sheep. Then Jacob kissed Rachel and began to weep aloud." (Genesis 29: 10b-11, NIV) Jacob and Rachel had an instant love connection.

Jacob had searched hard and long for a wife and found Rachel on his trip to Laban's terrain. Laban had two daughters, Leah who was the older and weaker one and Rachel the youngest was the beautiful one. Jacob knew immediately that he was in love with Rachel and told Laban: "I'll work for you seven years in return for your younger daughter Rachel." (Genesis 29:18)

Jacob discovered after seven years of working and waiting that Laban had deceived him. Laban did not keep his word to Jacob asserted that he was already married to Leah. Though Jacob was married to Leah, he still wanted Rachel. Jacob agreed to work for Laban seven more years and was married to both Leah and Rachel. "When the Lord saw that Leah was not loved, he enabled her to conceive, but Rachel remained childless." (Genesis 29:31)

Many people think that certain things are simply easy. To some a *wife is a wife*, a *job is a job* and so on. Some Christians even believe that a *church is a church*. These individuals do not see the reason for driving across town to a particular place of worship. A person with such an attitude does not understand what real destiny is. The right connection to the right person is what makes a relationship work. Ruth had to be connected to Boaz to make it just as Jacob had to be connected with Rachel to fulfill God's will of giving birth to Joseph.

Jacob was compelled by God to work another seven years for Rachel. He knew in his heart that Rachel was an important part of his destiny. The predictive wisdom instilled in him had persuaded him that Rachel was the right choice for a wife. You must think like Jacob and have a sense of destiny! Just as Leah may have been able to give him many children Rachel only gave him one who would become important to the entire family later. Someone or something in your life may provide you with plenty of things but your blessing may come from the one who appears to have the least to offer.

Additional Stress

Just as Rachel had to wait fourteen years to marry her true love we sometimes have to wait for our true blessing. This is where hope falls into play. Rachel experienced some of her most stressful years waiting for Jacob, and again waiting for children. That same stress happens in many of our lives, from one disappointment to another, we find ourselves waiting for relief. While Leah was producing plenty of children for Jacob, Rachel was waiting on God for one! It is stressful to wait and like Rachel many of you have experienced the stress of waiting for something you believe you are long overdue for. It could be a good woman, or a good man, a good job, a new house, a well needed car, and more.

Have you become angry, frustrated and or even depressed over waiting for something? Whatever you do, never give up. Hold on to your faith and your hope in God. He will turn things around and bless you for your patience. Just as God caused and allowed stress to come to Jacob and Rachel in waiting for each other, He blessed them with Joseph. He may allow some stress in your life to bless you with success in the end.

Often when nothing seems to be happening is when God is working behind the scenes. You can't see it but, many times God is working out the condition for the position He wants to see you in. God's sovereignty is at work when we are completely unaware of its presence. Anyway I tell you that just like Abraham waited twenty five years before Sarah became pregnant and gave birth to their first child, Joseph endured thirteen years of betrayal, imprisonment, and abandonment before becoming the leader of Egypt, Moses spent forty years as a sheepherder before God called him to a greater purpose of saving His people, David waited fourteen years for the throne of Israel to become his, and Jesus waited until His hour came.

Stress is associated with waiting. Consider all of those who have waited before you. They each had restraint in the opposition of oppression. Maintain a spiritual posture called longsuffering and know that it is the grace of God that compels you to trust Him. Sometimes the stress of waiting is intense but your role in the battle is to persevere by expanding your knowledge in Him so that He can complete your faith.

"Those who hope in me will not be disappointed"
(Isaiah 49:23, NIV).

Job: Unwavering Faith

Job is another man of the Bible who endured much stress. Job's life is described as that of a great person of faith. The Bible describes Job as a man who loved God and was obedient to Him. The Bible tells us that

Job was blameless, "There was a man in the land of Uz, whose name was Job; and that man was perfect and upright, and one that feared God, and eschewed evil." (Job 1:1, KJV). Although Job lived a life that pleased God, the Lord allowed a devastating situation to overwhelm him. Satan was allowed to test him.

The first test was for Job to accept the loss of his possessions and descendants (Job 1:6-22). The second test was to endure losing his health (Job 2:1-10).The third test was to withstand false accusations. The criteria for Job's test were to bear it all without sinning or blaming God. God allowed each test.

In the first test God allowed Satan to take away all of Job's possessions. Satan tested Job by taking away all of his possessions. Satan took all of his herds and property. Satan thought that if he took away all of Job's wealth, Job would reject God, but Job remained faithful (1-22). Instead after the tragedies struck, Job tore his robe and shaved his head.

God reaffirms to Satan that Job truly loves God and all the ways of God. Satan's second test was allowed by God with the instruction to touch his flesh but not his life (2:6). Satan tormented Job by bringing afflictions upon his entire body. Job was struck with boils from head to toe (2:7). The afflictions were so bad that Job's wife told him to curse God and die (2:9). But, Job declared his wife to be a foolish woman and he never lost hope. Job refused to speak against God.

The third test, God allowed Satan to torment Job even further. Job was emotionally alone, suffering pain and anxiety. He was confused and angry when Satan had three of his friends, Eliphaz the Temanite, Bildad the Shuhite, and Zophar the Naamathite verbally persecute him. These three men accused Job of being a malicious sinner. They had initially come to Job to comfort him. But, when they saw him, they found it hard to believe it was Job.

Eliphaz, Bildad, and Zophar wept out loud, tore their robes and sat silently with Job for seven days (2:13). In his frustration, Job cursed the day he was born. He wished to die. His friends were concerned about him. Yet, they still tormented him with accusations of sinning. They believed that his afflictions were a curse because of him sinning and demanded that he confess.

Job was stressed and at his lowest point of suffering. Yet, he still prayed. He had been deprived of all of his possessions, his descendants, and his health. Job's wife had also given up on him and wished for him to die too. He had been false accused of evil deeds by his most trusted friends. All of his self-esteem and strength was destroyed. Job's heart was broken without any explanation of why these things had happened to him. Job appealed to God to end his suffering. God had not even spoken to him during these tests. Job assumed God was persecuting him but he didn't know why.

In Chapter 38 of Job, God showed up. While, Jobs friends were taking action against him, God was taking action for him and revealed himself. In Chapter 42 of Job, he recognized God's presence, His knowledge and His power and he repented for doubting God (42:6). In His wrath, God spoke to Job's three friends about the lies concerning His existence. God commanded them to make a sacrifice for themselves to Him of seven bulls and seven rams (Job 42:7, 8). Job prayed for his friends. God acknowledged his prayer. He blessed Job by restoring his possessions twofold (Job 42:12, 13).

Job's life story provides an example for everyone everywhere. We learn through suffering that the sovereignty of God has its ultimate purpose. We see that suffering can come "overnight" (1:13-19) to anyone regardless of how righteous he or she may be. Job's tests confirm that Christians must be prepared for trials. The book of James tells us that "Yet you do not know what your life will be like tomorrow. You are just a vapor that appears for a little while and then vanishes away" (James 4:14).

Job's story showed that friends and family cannot always be relied upon (2:9-13). Our faith in God needs to be like Job's and expressed to other Christians throughout the world. Only obedience to the Lord will lead to a successful outcome for his children in times of tribulation.

Obstacles Before Miracles

When I first became a Christian, I wanted to speed up on building a close relationship with God, so I ran through the Bible and through my study of the Scriptures. I was excited about praying and being a part of the Christian experience. Everyone in church looked so beautiful and they all seemed so pleasant to be around.

However, little did I know that nicer people were outside of the church. When I went to Sunday school I gained the critics eye when I noticed one individual seeking more attention than the other. At choir rehearsals, I noticed that special people received the lead parts. Then at the church's annual meetings I noticed that officers were not selected based on what they could do but rather on how long they had been at the church, how wealthy they were, and who they knew.

Christianity was beginning to have the appearance of a sorority or social club organization. Where are the faith and the Christ like attitudes I expected to see in the church? For me and I am sure for many others Christianity had become a routine place for societal opponents. My journey started out being very happy to take the leap of faith to wanting to run as fast as I could for cover. Just as I was preparing to make my grand exit the chair person from one of the church's auxiliaries approached me. She asked spoke to me about speaking at the Women's Day Program. I said yes because I believed Jesus was still there and I didn't want to be defeated by the Devil's wicked scheme. God is and always was in control.

For some reason I knew that there was a lesson in this experience for me as well as for the people of this church. However at this time I wasn't sure what the lesson was. As time went on I gained a wealth of knowledge about church folk. Every pastor, ministry leader, and church goer gets educated on what a negative church person is.

Guess Who's Coming to Church?

Let me be more specific about negative church folks. I am talking about the person who is negative about everything and everybody in the church. The one who shows up at every Sunday service, serves as a member of every auxiliary and gives above and beyond their 10%. But, what is this person's true motive? This person is suspicious of the leadership of the church, the ministry, the sermons, the money and the very words written in the church bulletins. But they adore the windows in the sanctuary because they purchased most of them. Do you get the picture?

Negativity comes from the most unexpected sources. It is not always the flamboyant lady up front with the big hat. She just likes showing off her hats. It's not always the person who sings the loudest or shouts out loud. They are just happy to be in the service. Many times it is that quiet little lady or man, who thinks that his or her status and time in the church has bought them privileges. These can be some of the most annoying people you ever encounter.

Put On Your Armor of God

Before you grab a hot skillet or pot of grits from the stove make sure you put on your mitt. Deal with your sins before you address others. Make sure that you are right before you consider what they are upset about is wrong. It is a good practice for a Christian leader to analyze themselves first. We must Biblically humble ourselves according to God's Word. We are human and capable of human error the same as anyone else. Romans 12: 3 said "Do not think of yourself more highly than you ought..."

Our natural tendency is to view church leaders from the wrong perspective... We place them on a pedestal as super heroes and this becomes a major problem in our churches. As Christian we are all leaders and have some type of influence on the life of someone else. So we all need to know how to behave according to God. We are teammates the work of God. Paul insists that all Christians should work together for one purpose. In 2 Corinthians 3:8 he said "Will not the ministry of the Spirit have even more glory? For if there was glory in the ministry of condemnation, the ministry of righteousness must far exceed it in glory."

What Paul was telling us is that no single leader is sufficient to help a church prosper. It takes many individuals with different skills and strengths. No one individual can bear all of the pressure and spiritual warfare that comes upon a church. And every member of a church including the leader needs someone to help them stay focused.

The Bible makes it clear that each of us is a sinner and everyone we have a relationship with is also. Because of that conflict is inevitable. Our attitudes and emotions are always under attack; however, God calls for us to grow in grace. Whether we are the offended or the offender, we are instructed by Christ to "Let all bitterness and wrath and anger and clamor and slander be put away from you, along with all malice" (Ephesians 4:31, ESV).

My Leap of Faith

It was a chilly Sunday afternoon at Zion Baptist Church in Canton, Georgia. January 21, 2012 was the exact date. I had been at the church since moving to Canton in November of 2011. It felt great being in a smaller church where people could actually meet and get to know each other. I had spent so many years in the larger congregations with thousands of people who rarely knew each other's name. Many of them came to church because it was the thing to do and it was where people of a certain status attended.

Zion Baptist Church often had dinner following the worship service and my husband James and I would attend. Who would turn down some good old "Soul Food?" This Sunday the church had arranged for a lovely dinner in the downstairs dining hall. We filled our plates and spotted a table near the exit door that was not too crowed. I asked if we could occupy the empty seats. Very quickly I could tell that we were sitting with a family and friends group who had been around the church since its inception.

Everyone already knew who we were and asked numerous questions about what brought us to Zion, where we lived, worked, and family. I didn't have to ask anyone who they were or how long they had been at the church because a very kind lady at the table Mrs. Pitts made a point of letting me know that her family had a long history at the church and she went on to introduce James and me to the people around the table.

Just as I was about to give up on God he presents me with a challenge. I was ready to exit this Christian scene based on what I had seen over the last few months, however, God had other plans. Sometimes unexpected events drive us to make commitments we normally wouldn't contemplate. This move was designed by God to take me from fear to hopefulness. Mrs. Pitts informed me that she was the Chairperson for the Women's Auxiliary of the church. Later during the conversation she asked if I would be the Keynote speaker for the church's Women's Day Program. Reluctantly, I said "Yes."

In just a few minutes I had met six important members of the Zion Baptist Church and the Canton community. I learned that one of the ladies at the table was the sister and sister-in-laws of Mrs. Pitts. The two men at the table were their husbands. Mrs. Pitts stated that she remembered from my initial introduction and was impressed by the way I carried myself even though I had all that education and experience. Mrs. Pitts felt my speaking would be a good way to get me involved with church activities and allow me to meet people in the community who would be attending.

I could see the closeness as the family lovingly gazed at each other as they laughed and talked about their experiences growing up. They had all attended Zion since they were children and had seen the church go through many transitions. In fact the dining hall was named in honor of Mr. Pitts, late husband of Mrs. Pitts, who had served as a highly recognized and respected deacon before his death. This family appeared to be very close and I could see by the way they laughed and talked with one another that they spent a lot of time together. James and I were the new kids on the block and were honored to have been allowed to sit with such pleasant people. They were much different from the other group we met a few weeks early.

As we were leaving the church one of the members of the other highly recognized families met us at the exit. "Dr. Sullivan, you are welcome to join us anytime" She said and gave me her business card as she walked away. Just as we prepared to exit the building she turned to me again and said, "I know you are new to the area and may not know your way around. Call me if you need some help." We thanked her and proceeded on our destination home. I was moved by the kindness from all of the people of Zion at this point.

The next Sunday at Church Mrs. Pitts was ushering and was the first face we saw as we entered. She was usually smiling, but this time her facial expression was a little saddened. I spoke with her later and learned that the two groups did not have a good relationship and she did not want me to get caught up in the middle of church mess. I thanked her for the warning and assured her that I am not a trouble maker but a problem solver. I did find out over time that she was right and numerous people were using all types of manipulative tactics to gain favor.

I found this out when the church experienced the loss of our Senior Pastor. After an unfavorable situation caused the interim pastor to leave the church, I became the provisional pastor until one could be selected. This was a position which placed me in the middle of the storm because I was the only ordained and licensed minister who had membership with the church. I was only there to serve until the church could find a suitable pastor, one group wanted to use me against the other. What a stressful experience. However, God has a plan.

My heart was saddened by what I had seen and experienced from these so called Christians. In a little under two years at this church, I witnessed more negativity than I had ever seen in the streets or in the penal institution I had worked in. These people did everything but fist fight. My heart was heavy and my spirit was wounded. I kept wondering, "What is it you want me to learn God?" I never questioned Him though, I just continued on with my Heavenly Father's work.

I could not turn my back on God, so being the compassionate person I am, I went on preaching and trying to council as many people as I could to get them to understand that this building or status they were fighting over was separating them from God's love and from the love of one another. I was determined to help them understand that it was not about them but about *Him*. I finally found the right opportunity to take a punch at sin. I took the opportunity on Sunday, January 13, 2013 in morning service to preach a sermon titled *Get You House in Order*. My heart and my thoughts were working overtime.

This church had allowed the Devil to set up fulltime residency and I was determined to teach them how to rebuild their spiritual homes. I needed to do this and I went forward with faith that God would be with me. That Sunday I preached this sermon I could see the facial expressions from the pulpit. The people were so shocked that I would speak on their character or their church but no one said a word. Mrs. Pitts and other key members of the church looked at me with utter surprise and stared intently at me as I spoke.

My sermon began by telling them what the Bible said about a house divided. The Bible states "And if a house be divided against itself, that house cannot stand" (Mark 3:25). They needed to hear this because it was unacceptable to have groups and clicks fighting in the House of the Lord. I also discussed what the book of Acts. These people were glorifying the building and their positions instead of glorifying God. "The Lord of heaven and earth does not live in temples built by man hands" (Acts 17:24). The Bible also tells us that where two or more are gathered, God is with them (Matthew 18:20 NIV).

I was angry with the way they were treating each other and for their lack of respect for God and His people. I told them that I was troubled by their actions and how they may affect other new comers and babes in Christ. Many eyes were filled with tears and some faces were filled with anger because they had been exposed. Mrs. Pitts sat up a bit taller and boldly stated at the end of service that she got the message.

By this time I knew that I had gained new friends and enemies, however, that didn't matter because God's Word had spoken for itself.

Bit by bit the word of God was fed to a starving people. They all needed a deeper understanding of God's faithfulness and of His purpose for the church. I closed with Psalm which states "Except the Lord build the house, they labor in vain that build it" (Psalm 127:1, KJV).

What I know for sure is that we cannot be saved without faith (John 3:36), we cannot live without faith (1 John 5:4) and we cannot please God without faith (Hebrew 11:6). Faith in God is essential in every situation. I stepped out on faith to deal with this situation. On February 27, 2013, James and I, left Zion Baptist Church and moved to Hoover, Alabama. When we left Georgia the two groups at Zion Baptist Church were still at war. I recently received word, one group had left and started a church. I left knowing that I had "stepped out on faith" and told them what God expects of them. Do not be held hostage by sin and wickedness, but know that the Kingdom of faith is the home of every Christian.

In a parable, Jesus cautioned Christians to be on guard and not allow evil to permeate us (Matthew 16:6-12). In another parable, He taught how the mustard seed that the church will start out small and later grow to great magnitudes. However, birds will come to nest in the church. Birds represented evil. He explained that we will never be free of evil forces but they do not have to corrupt or discourage us because we are the seeds of wheat that remain and Jesus is the Sower and Harvester of our faith (Matthew 13:31-32). We are encouraged in the book of Hebrews to "fix our eyes on Jesus who is the author and finisher of our faith" (Hebrews 12:2).

Chapter 5

The Christian Response to Despair

My first experience with despair was in October 1999 when my husband and I received the news that he had prostate cancer that had advanced to his glands. I had experience from being with many church friends and members during sad times but was not prepared for my own personal journey through despair.

My husband had decided to follow the advice of a friend he had spoken with at one of our Eastern Kentucky reunions. My handsome husband had gone to the doctor just to take a simple PSA test since he was at the age where men should start taking precautions. A few days after the exam we received the word firsthand from his doctor. The situation seemed grim. He had just lost his father and his sister from cancer and it was shocking to hear that he had the same disease.

My emotional state could be described as fearful and depressed. I had been discouraged before and even depressed about inconsequential things like passing an exam, missing a flight, relationship problems, and even passing my doctoral defense. Here was another thing I had no control of.

I had experienced the loss of my grandparents and other relatives. In fact, I had officiated at a few funerals and served in many other home going ceremonies to sing or pray. The most emotional funeral I participated in was for my Head Pastor where I was asked by the family to deliver the family prayer. In the short time we had been there the pastor and I had grown very close. We spoke often on Sunday nights after service and I learned many lessons about delivering God's word to the people from him and about being a good servant. I had just been informed by him that he was retiring and wanted me to serve as Associate Pastor to his son in his absence. He passed away a few days following my appointment. His death was hard on the entire congregation and God helped me to focus on providing comfort and encouragement to the church and to the Pastor's family. The work I had to do along was my help through the challenges ahead was intense but nothing like the experience of watching my husband go through the painful process of cancer treatments.

The situation with James was different. He was my husband, my friend, and my helpmate. He was only 49 and we had so much to do. Statistically with his father, sister, and other family members dying from cancer his life span was reduced. I was consumed by the possibility of his death. It took all that was in me not to drown in a pool of depression and hopelessness.

At first, James seemed traumatized by the news of cancer. His expression reflected fear and gloom. I remember seeing that look many times. My mother had a similar expression for each of her parents and I had seen many church members and friends and relatives at the end of their lives display it too. Finding the right words to say to someone when they receive sad news is not easy. But there is comfort in God's word.

Mr. James Sullivan Jr., My husband, My friend!

An Emotional Disabler

Not many things can disable us emotionally like death and despair. However, the Bible has several verses that tell us what to do when we are faced with such matters. The Scripture says, "Delight yourself in the Lord and He will give you the desires of your heart" (Psalms 37:4 NIV). That doesn't mean God will bring back the loved one you lost or heal you from cancer. But it does mean that He will do what is best for you. He will give you the strength to withstand any situation.

I can attest to this because of what God has done in my life. He showed favor by healing James of cancer, not once but twice. Also by, delivering me from the bondage of those days I felt unloved and unwanted growing up. God always stepped in and showed me that my life was worth something when I felt like throwing in the towel. The faithfulness of God gave me the strength to arrive where I am today. Without His faithfulness this book would not be possible. God has given me what I desired. The more we trust in God the closer we become to having the desires of our heart fulfilled.

Everyone who lives Godly must suffer. However, God never goes back on His promises. "God is not human, that he should lie, not a human being, that he should change his mind. Does he speak and then not act? Does he promise and not fulfill" (Numbers 23:19). Sometimes during our despair we lose faith. When we need to be inspired the Scripture reminds us that God is always near. If we look back over our lives, we will find that He does what he said He would do. Man may fail you, but God never fails.

When you are going through hardships or grieving, you can always turn to the Bible for help. When we reach out to God to help us through challenging times, it is comforting to learn that you are not alone; God has comforted many people of faith. The Psalms are filled with many verses that represent pleas to God to remember His people in times of despair. The psalmist testifies to the transforming power of God. One of the most comforting verses for me refers to God's ability to turn "mourning into dancing" (Psalms 30:8-12).

Many people experience despair and emotional disorders related to life-changing experiences, illness, and death. These conditions leave people feeling hopeless and in need of psychological help. Doctors and mental health professionals are recognizing spiritually as a central component of psychological well-being.

Many people turn to medical doctors for answers to their problems, "but others find support through their spiritual beliefs outside the context of organized religion" (McClain, Rosenfeld, & Breitbart, 2003). In relation to terminally ill patients, no specific link has been assessed between spiritual well-being and end of life despair. But a link between depression, desire to hasten death, suicidal ideation, and hopelessness has consistently been seen in studies related to medically-ill and terminally-ill people (McClain, Rosenfeld, & Breitbart, 2003).

Although relatively little data exists about the role religion plays in the lives of mentally ill people. In an annotated bibliography Peteet (2007) calls for clinicians to find ways of using religious resources for healing. Kirov, Kemp, Kirov, *et al* (1998) performed a study of 52 patients in a psychiatric facility about their religious beliefs. More than 66% were religious and over 20% said religion was the most essential part of their lives; 30.4 % had increased their religiousness since becoming ill, and 61.2% used religion as a coping mechanism.

In a study by Dell (2004); the backgrounds, education, training, and roles of religious professionals were reviewed to distinguish between the characteristics of counseling. The areas of counseling reviewed were faith-based counseling in churches, hospitals and by psychiatric chaplaincy. Dell encourages health professionals and religious professionals to collaborate to offer more practical requirements for care of child and adolescent patients.

Christians and Depression

Years ago, I worked at a juvenile facility as a counselor. A student explained that she had been depressed because she didn't feel she could do anything right. I would tell her that she was a beautiful girl and assured her that whoever told her that was actually the one with the problem. Unaware of just how severe this young lady's problems were, I was quickly blew her off each time she wanted to talk. A few months after release from the facility, the young lady committed suicide. She left a note to her parents apologizing for not making them happy.

Never again, will I ignore the voice of someone crying out for help. I take depression very seriously. I know from my own thoughts of harming myself as a teenager that this is a dangerous state to be in. During my youth, when I was afraid to go to sleep because I thought my grandmother was going to kill me or simply feared a beating I didn't know what depression was. I simply thought I was a curse and embarrassment to my family.

In some religious circles, depression is considered demon possession and must be cured through exorcism or prayer. Many depressed people are criticized and considered to be lacking in faith. I can assure you that most people who attempt harm to themselves or others suffer from something much deeper than what meets the human eye.

Depression can be spiritually induced by guilt, a sense of failure, fear, and death. The Scriptures make specific disciplines available for these situations (Jeremiah 8:22). We often ignore the fact that our physiological state affects our spiritual and psychological state of mind. In 1Kings 19, Elijah was afraid and worn out from struggling to defeat Jezebel. He was so depressed that he cried out to God "take my life"... (I Kings 19:4).

The Lord sent a message by His angel telling Elijah to get up have some food and he was strengthened and rested for the night. Then Elijah was sent back out to do the will of God. Christians know comfort may be gained in taking our burdens to God; however we learned from the Scripture that He recommends food and sleep. He will give us rest through our obedience.

> "Come to me, all you who are weary and burdened, and I will give you rest" (Matthew 11:28 NIV).

How Does Depression Feel?

Depression occurs for a variety of reasons and is an extremely complex disease. Some people become depressed because of medical illness and others become depressed because of trauma or serious life changing circumstances. Yet there are others who have a genetic history of depression in their family or experience depression for no known reason.

Depression may be the result of a chemical imbalance in the body. For over three decades, scientists have attributed chemical imbalance as a source of major depression that impacts 5% of people globally (Nauert, 2006).

It is possible to develop depression with or without one or more of the following: a family history of mental health, chronic physical or mental disorders, major life changes and stress, lack of support, psychological factors, and low socioeconomic status, based on gender, age, sleep disorders, or medication. However, several known factors increase the chances for depression.

Factors such as (1) abuse related to past physical, sexual, or emotional abuse, (2) adverse reaction to certain medications can increase the risk of depression, (3) personal conflicts or disputes may trigger a vulnerable person into depression, (4) sadness or grief related to the loss of a loved one may increase the threat of depression.

Emotional Lockdown

No matter what you do, things don't change. Life is sometimes like pressing the repeat button over and over again. You continue to replay things from the past and you end up feeling angry with other people or at yourself. You are now on emotional lockdown. Thoughts of anger and self- hatred are associated with feelings of guilt and self-blame. Your mind becomes trapped in a painful state. The process of thinking is delayed and painful. You become overwhelmed by uncertainty and illogical thoughts.

Depression brings about feelings inadequacy and hopelessness which may lead to an individual becoming inactive. The person becomes trapped in a negative state of mind. Imagine being an athlete sitting on the bench waiting for your term to play but never getting called. Game after game you wait but each game the coach leaves you out. You begin to feel sad and low in spirit. The person repeatedly thinks about giving up or contemplating some alternative route of achieving satisfaction.

This is where an individual's thinking becomes defective. He or she may have crying spells, contemplate suicide, or seek pleasure in unhealthy activities. A depressed person feels hopeless and has recurrent negative thoughts that something is missing inside of him or her. Changes in behavior may range from appetite disorders to sleep disorders. From a psychoanalytic perspective, a depressed individual may recall fears, losses, and memories from the past. It may be useful to know what happens in the brain during depression.

A group of researchers used a new holistic approach to investigate the functional connectivity changes in the brains of people suffering with major depression. According to Tao, Guo, Ge, Kendrick, Xue, Liu and Feng (2013). The holistic approach was adopted to identify the altered circuits in the brains of depressed people unlike other approaches which assume that the brain an mental illness are independent of one another. Tao *et. al.* argued that changes in the brains functional circuit may alter both positive and negative correlations in the brain thus affecting the hate circuits in the brains of depressed people ((pg108).

The main focus of their study was to identify the altered pathways in first-episode major depressive disorder (FEMDD) and resistant major depressive disorder (RMDD) patients suffering from depression to establish the linkage per se. The researchers implied that "the 'hate circuit' may be involved in the control of other behaviors influenced by depression." (pg. 109) These same regions of the brain are associated with feelings of self-awareness. It is acknowledged that we need a better understanding of how mental depression alters the brain functions.

Because of the physical and emotional changes you normally become more irritable to people around you. Your body pains tend to intensify as well as your loss of desire for social interaction. Concentration on work may become difficult and you may begin to use alcohol or drugs to numb the pain, however, you only make matters worse.

Mental health (2012) presented a worldwide statistical overview of mental health facts. More than 450 million people worldwide have mental health problems. Depression is the leading cause of disability and will be the single biggest medical burden by the year 2020. Globally 20 % of those with mental disorders are children and adolescents. Ninety percent of the individuals who die of suicide in the Western countries have mental illness. Asia has the smallest proportion of mentally ill individuals. In 2006 a survey revealed that 95% of the homicides were related to people with undiagnosed mental illness.

In other words, if you are experiencing any of the symptoms mentioned earlier in this chapter, you may be depressed. Almost everyone who is depressed complained about anger, guilt, loss, sadness or other emotions. Often individuals do not realize that they are depressed and it has been established by (Kendler, Karkowski, & Prescott, 1999) that a stressful life may cause the onset of depressive episodes. The use of religious coping strategies has been the focus of recent research.

Religion as a Coping Mechanism for Depression

Over the past decade, positive and negative religious coping strategies have been used to predict mental health outcomes. Despite the findings, many researchers realize the need for more studies to explain causational and interpretational uncertainties related to coping with depression (Carpenter, Laney, & Mezulis, 2011). Carpenter implied that religious coping may be moderate depending on factors such as global location and religious commitment of the individual. Numerous studies have found that global indices of religiosity. The findings of this study revealed that there is a causal link between depressive symptoms and global religiosities such as prayer. Depression along with positive and negative mental health outcomes have all been explained in cross-sectional research.

The Bible doesn't use the word "depression," but it does describe many people who displayed the symptoms of depression. The Bible does not refer to psychotropic medications or antidepressants either. However, the Scripture does provide guidelines and principles for dealing with specific ailments. The Scripture refers to issues of sin and conflict and many other problems that may affect ones emotional state.

A Christian's life is based on fact and not on feelings. Philippians 4 instructs us to rejoice in the Lord in all things. In Matthew 10:1, Jesus orders His Disciples to become healers of all matter of diseases. And though the Scripture does not use the word "depression", God's Word has plenty to say about dealing with discouragement and despair. We have also heard from various researchers that severe depression can lead to other physical and psychological disorders. In addition to seeking biblical help I encourage anyone suffering from depression to seek the guidance of medical and mental health professionals.

The Scripture provides several relevant verses telling us what we can do to help with depression and other stressful situations. Proverbs 13:12 said that hope deferred makes the heart sick, but when the desire comes it is a tree of life. Proverbs 18:14 tells us that the human spirit can endure a sick body, but who can bear it if the spirit is crushed? During Job's challenging moments he responded by saying ""My days are swifter than a weaver's shuttle, and are spent without hope... "Therefore I will not restrain my mouth; I will speak in the anguish of my spirit; I will complain in the bitterness of my soul." (Job 7:6, 11).

When we become depressed and hopeless the Bible commands us to put on the whole armor of God. The Ephesians encouraged us to faithfully trust God with everything concerning our lives. The Scripture lets us know that God's power is stronger than anything we face.

Put on the whole armor of God,
that you may be able to stand against the wiles of the devil.
For we do not wrestle against flesh and blood,
but against principalities, against powers,
against the rulers of the darkness of this age,
against spiritual hosts of wickedness in the heavenly places
(Ephesians 6:11-12).

Satan wants you to fail and to give up and he will throw as many negative thoughts and tricks as possible toward us. But, God wants us to be encouraged. We must guard our thoughts and seek God's help. And though our human nature doesn't want to acknowledge the need for help, God tells us to seek Him when we are depressed. God can and will give us peace of heart and minds. In Psalms 31:23-24 David lets us know that the Lord loves us and encourages every Christian to be strengthened by his or her hope in the Lord.

A Christian Reaction

Christian's lives like all others can be capsized. When struggle takes place between faith and hope it's as if a collision occurred at a spiritual amusement park. These are real life experiences can make one feel completely out of control. When things don't happen as expected and circumstances seem gloomy, disappointment steps in to steal whatever is left of our joy. But, Christians there is a solution ahead called relief.

The Christian's Journey to Relief

When things go wrong, us Christians battle with feelings of disappointment. Many times we may become angry with God for letting bad things happen. Similar, to Peter who reminded Jesus that he and his people had left everything to follow Him (Mark 10:28-30). And things were not going as expected. Perhaps, you feel the same way.

Thinking that we have made the sacrifice to become a Christian yet bad things still happen to us. We wonder what we're doing wrong. And, why loss and disappointments still come. It may be that we are taking the wrong approach finding relief from our distress.

It's okay to be disappointed and angry but God wants us to handle our disappointments a certain way. Instead of "giving up" and "giving in" to the issues faced, He wants us to bring all of our problems to Him. Jesus has the answer that we seek and provides the guidelines telling us to:

Endure: James encourages us to remain hopeful (James 1:1-4).

James encourages us to stay hopeful with "count it all joy" when we face trials and tests. As we endure, we will emerge complete and lacking nothing. God allows us to go through things to shape our character and prepare us for receiving what He has prepared for us. It may be hard, but even in our pain we must find the strength to continue trusting, praying, and believing in God's promises. Jesus said to call upon Him when you have trouble: "I will deliver thee, and thou shalt glorify me" (Psalms 50:15).

Seek Wisdom: James encourages us to stop worrying and seek God's help (James 1:5).

Ask God for wisdom concerning problems faced. James encouraged us to activate our faith expecting God to answer. In Jeremiah, Jesus said, "Call to Me, and I will answer you, and I will tell you great and mighty things, which you do not know" (Jeremiah 33:3). He promises to enlighten us with knowledge and show us how to deal with our problems.

Trust God: James tells us to come to God with a faithful heart (James 1:6-8).

Go to God remembering that He is holy and He is faithful. Asking God for help is very important in your relationship with Him. When you ask God for help you are saying that you trust Him. Just as Peter did when Jesus allowed him to walk on water, you must surrender all to Him. "So humble yourselves under the mighty power of God, and at the right time he will lift you up in honor. Give all your worries and cares to God, for he cares about you" (1 Peter 5:6-7). Paul tells us to have faith for, "Without faith it is impossible to please God..." (Hebrews 11:6, NIV). The Bible encourages Christians to build their faith. The Scriptures states:

"But you, dear friends, by building yourselves up in your most holy faith and praying in the Holy Spirit, keep yourselves in God's love as you wait for the mercy of our Lord Jesus Christ to bring you to eternal life" (Jude 1:20-23, NIV).

Godly men and women exercise faith in their lives by trying to duplicate a "Christ like spirit" in everything they do. Exercising faith releases a power in man that leads him to serving God in his daily practices. Christian men and women who truly aim to serve are obedient in practicing His ways and in loving his or her fellow man. Serving God establishes our faith.

Chapter 6

Connections

We have all kinds of connections through the different people in our lives. Yet, many people feel disconnected below the surface level. Does anyone really know whom he or she is connected to and just what that connection is? For some people, the only connection they know is physical. Others are just for a season. Some are more than blood ties - spiritually designed by God to accomplish His plan for our lives.

Such a connection is very important and comes with a deep-longing to be in His presence. Most people claim to believe in God. Yet, many do not know how to connect with Him. Many people are just looking for love and acceptance. Many cousins and good buddies suddenly appear. However, with God there is a distinct difference. You will learn more of this type as you read on about my nephew Paul Gaffney.

Paul, a retired member of the famous Harlem Globetrotters, professional exhibition basketball team, CEO and Founder of The Chattanooga Railrunners an affiliate of the (CBA) Central Basketball Association. Aside from being running this professional men's basketball team, Paul is a faithful servant of God and a loving family man. He prioritizes his connections in the right order. Paul invigorated my soul when I asked him to share with me his true feelings on being adopted. First, he wanted me to know that God was first and foremost in his life, and family, profession, and business followed.

My connection with Paul is through the "blood of his mother" and the "blood of Jesus." Paul, my nephew, was given up for adoption at birth. As he openly and honestly shared his feelings about it, he admitted, "I was irritated that I lived so close to my "birth family" my entire early life. Yet, no one ever thought of telling me the truth of the situation. Now in my 40s, what can I tell my wife and children about my life and relatives? How do I stay strong for them? Was putting me up for adoption fair?" His voice was not filled with anger, confusion, or fear. But, a sincere yearning for truth.

Residing nearby, gave me the opportunity to see Paul grow up. I always knew that he was a pleasant and strong-minded young man. He enjoyed playing sports, encouraging other children, and making them laugh. He was raised in a very loving household where the Word of God was taught and practiced.

His first encounter with heartache was the loss of his father. The heartache involved the loss of a parent, a friend. But the deeper loss for Paul centered on the one true place he had been able to go for refuge for over 30 years. His dad was the one connection that God used to give him hope. He had married and found a place of comfort and love with his wife and in-laws but still there was the void of losing someone so dear. Gradually the pain faded and turned into joy. His connections with God came via his loving wife, two beautiful children, college friends, and friends he met in the business world and professional career with the Harlem Globetrotters.

The thought crossed my mind: He will be okay. Why open the door to things he was not aware of? If he opens his heart to new emotions, surely, he'd battle with far more than being adopted. He would face many unpleasant stories about his birth mother and grandparents. And grapple with questions he never had the courage to ask about his parents, himself, and God's plan for his life.

Peaks and Valleys of Emotions

Our lives are linked by numerous peaks and valleys. We often encounter situations that are over the top with joy and excitement. However, an occasional burst of havoc is wreaked on our emotions leaving us in a cesspool of emotional debris. Often we feel hopeless and distant from God. We are often caught between the extremes of our emotional highs and lows.

Peaks are like our emotions being projected to the highest points. Varying, in intensity and mystery. They rise giving us the most rewarding feeling of accomplishment that later narrows down to a platform level known as reality. At this level, we realize the designs of life are often shifting in another direction.

Valleys appear as life shifts back and forth. These emotional shifts are faced by most of us at various intervals in our lives. Our self-destruct mode may be from an unpleasant event that may have directed us to this level in life I refer to as "a valley". Many people journey for long periods in the valley. However, there is a way out. I thought to myself, "Paul must know the secret of navigating through these peaks and valleys."

Managing Difficult Emotions

Paul's ability to manage his emotions was much better than mine. One reason why emotions are so difficult is that we are not all overly apprehensive about the feelings of pain and disappointment. No one wants to hurt or feel pain. The loss of something or someone overwhelms us with sadness. But in another sense, feelings of anxiety may precede feelings of hope.

Perhaps an explanation of Paul's emotions associated with numerous situations in his life will explain why people want to avoid painful situations and sometimes escape reality. He shared the Scripture below to help me understand that he is not saddened by being adopted because his adoption had placed him into a family of God. I was amazed to hear these words from such a young man. Paul shared being a child of God meant more to him than any other connection in his life.

> "We know that the whole creation has been groaning as in the pains of childbirth right up to the present time. Not only so, but we ourselves, who have the first fruits of the Spirit, groan inwardly as we wait eagerly for our adoption to son ship, the redemption of our bodies" (Romans 8:22-23).

Paul H. Gaffney was born in 1968 and adopted at birth by two elderly individuals who were never able to have children of their own. Paul's adoptive father and mother were in their 60s when they adopted him. Paul's adopted mother passed away in 1970 before he was even two years old and able to bond with her. Therefore, he has no memory of that relationship. However, Paul's adoptive father kept and raised him.

Paul's remembers his father telling him about sitting in a rocker holding him and praying to God for strength to care for a baby and making the commitment to take care of him until he was able to care for himself. Mr. Gaffney promised Paul as a little boy that he would never marry or have different women in his life.

As Paul and I continued to talk about his life he revealed that his father had told him the truth about his adoption. But, very little about the birth family. Paul only knew the family's name and that they lived nearby. In fact, they were in walking distance from his home. Paul stated that he remembers a woman and two children walking past his home on a regular basis. For some reason, he always wondered who they were. He expressed having a strong feeling every time he saw them. He felt a connection.

After a brief moment of silence, Paul said he often asked himself, "Why did she keep my sister and brother and not me." He went on to say, "Even though I wondered about my family, I knew that God was with me at all times. My feelings were not those of sadness, I just questioned why," he shared. He went on to say, "When I met my sibling, I was happy to know them, but I knew I was in the right place and with the right person. That feeling replaced any feeling of sadness in me," Paul continued. "Knowing that I was loved and wanted was the most fulfilling and wonderful feeling in the world."

Total Forgiveness

Paul didn't have a meaningful conversation with his birth mother until he was 24 four years old. In 1992, he married his wife Liska on his dad's birthday. Paul remembers his dad saying to Liska's parents, "Now I'm ready because I know he is in good hands." One year later in February of 1993, his dad passed away. A bit of agony shattered Paul's emotions. Yet, he knew that his father was far along in age and that his health was failing.

A year or so after dealing with the anguish of losing his father, he was faced with the decision of meeting and talking with his birth mother. He had been raised by such a remarkable father in a Christian home and knew about forgiveness. Paul's mother had moved to another state, shortly after graduating from high school and returned home for a Memorial Day visit. Little did she know, the young baby she had given up for adoption was not only fully grown man of God, he was a college graduate and married. Paul's mother heard that he was in town and wanted to explain why she had given him up and apologize for causing him pain.

Along with being married, Paul was also a professional athlete with the famous Harlem Globetrotters. And, he's the proud father of a two-year-old little girl. He told me that he was just as excited to meet with his mother and introduce her to his family, as she was to see him. He implied that this was one of the most powerful and meaningful emotions he had ever experienced. Paul said, "I told her, I don't hate you. I forgive you. I know that you were young and did what you had to do."

He said, "I told her that I was glad she gave me up because I had a good life. I was raised in a good home by a loving father. I also told her that that I wanted her to meet my wife and her granddaughter."

Paul remembers saying, "I love you" as the last words he said to his mother. I can only imagine the feelings that existed throughout their visit. Emotions must have ranged from those of pain, hurt, to sadness and joy. Just as Paul responded to his mother's request for forgiveness, he clung to his emotional strengths. This allowed him to overlook his pain and grant the gift of forgiveness.

Later in our conversation, Paul started remembering more about his father and his mother. We talked about the "peaks and valley emotions" of these relationships. Paul expressed being the son of Mr. Gaffney had been one of his "highest peaks" in life. Followed by marrying the love of his life and becoming a parent. He said, "Sure there have been valleys, but I didn't see them in that way because God was always there. I saw them as building blocks allowing me to transform into what God already planned." He continued by saying, "I can't deny that I have had all types of emotions throughout my life, but they were just questions." Paul then cited verses in 1 Thessalonians.

"We always thank God for all of you and continually mention you in our prayers. We remember before our God and Father

your work produced by faith, your labor prompted by love, and your endurance inspired by hope in our Lord Jesus Christ" (1 Thessalonians 1: 2-3, NIV).

Paul expressed an attitude of joy as he reflected on the memory of what his dad had said to his wife Liska's parents before he died. His birth mother passed away a few years later while he was in South Africa with the Harlem Globetrotters. He expressed that he was happy that he got to talk to her and let her know that he forgave her. We did not discuss his birth father and Paul says meeting his mother was enough. Mr. Gaffney was his father.

Consider Paul's pain. His father was an elderly man far into his 60s when he adopted him. He was also a committed elder of the church and all around good person. Everyone loved Mr. Gaffney. He had an "entire village" ready to help him raise Paul. But one day God said, "Ellis, you have done well, it's time to come home."

> *His lord said unto him, well done, thou good and faithful servant: thou hast been faithful over a few things, I will make thee ruler over many things: enter thou into the joy of thy lord"* (Matthew 25:21).

Mr. Gaffney did a splendid job of raising Paul. He could only say good things about his father in return. That is what has brought him peace. He had the choice to slump down in the "valley of self-pity" or to accept that God could have Him rise to the highest peaks life could offer him. Paul chose the latter. He knew that God had made the "Right Connection."

> *Great men are rarely isolated mountain peaks;*
> *they are the summits of ranges.*
> *- Thomas W. Higginson*

> *It's all about creation and surprise.*
> *It just needs to be appreciated and watered like flowers.*
> *You have to water flowers.*
> *These peaks will come again.*
> *- Sonny Rollins*

I am proud of the man You became!

Paul Gaffney

Chapter 7

While We Wait

I wasn't always the most patient in waiting. I sometimes thought I had my fair share of it. I spent all of my childhood waiting for my grandmother to love me, a part of my adult life waiting for people in my life to change, and many nights crying and praying as I waited for my children to all be saved and walk in grace. If there were a financial payment for patience I would be a millionaire, many times over.

Not many people enjoy waiting for something or somebody. However, in life most of us are forced to wait for the "wheels of life" to turn in the right direction. The use of the Internet, texting, and social media keeps us quickly connected to things and people without much waiting. Technology today allows us to shop, get directions, pay bills, work, and store records while in transit. High-speed forms of communication are steadily being built. Electronic books, games, videos, and even Bibles can be accessed in just a matter of seconds through notebooks note pads, eReader, and smartphones from most locations. Some of these very inventions have served as our worst enemies. Many users are so preoccupied with the latest mobile apps that they become completely unaware of their surroundings. Resulting in more and more distracted driving accidents and deaths. I can almost imagine God's thoughts about us giving so much power to technology the life of others can be endangered. As society becomes more easily distracted with "new gadgets" it is important to regain focus on what matters most – the Word of God.

I recently called a friend in Jamaica to request a reference letter be sent to a local college I was applying to work for. Even though he had to go to work that day, he still promised to send the college and myself the reference letter before noon my time. I had been on my computer just after noon. The letter never came across the nearby fax. I couldn't understand what had happened. I assumed it was the timeline difference or he got busy and forgot to send it.

Just after noon, I decided to give my friend a call. While we were on the phone, he walked over to his secretary's desk to confirm the letter had been sent. She assured him it had. In the meantime, I checked my email and fax once again but still no document. "Check your trash folder documents to see if it went there," he encouraged. I agreed and said I would give him a call back. I reluctantly checked the trash folder. Once on the computer, it crossed my mind that I hadn't received any new emails or faxes since the day before. That was strange. So, I decided to check my IPad to see if I could connect to my favorite game. No luck! After allowing frustration to get the best for a short while, I realized that my cable and Internet service didn't work. I called my cable provider and was informed that bad weather bought on a cable outage in the area. A service technician walked me through the rebooting process. Bam! Emails and faxes awaited. Through the day's difficulties, don't give up. There are solutions to every problem. And, even a greater likelihood that good news is ahead despite inconvenience and frustration you may have experienced.

The Frustration of life's Delays

Sometimes, we allow situations to frustrate us that we have absolutely no control of. A few weeks ago, I made a hair salon appointment, early on my least busy day of the week in hope of "getting in" and "out" in a reasonable amount of time. After all, I wanted to do a little "mall surfing" while in the area. So, I arrived early but for some reason still had a two-hour wait while the client in front of me, a lady with much money and power received preferential treatment. I was delayed for nearly five hours.

Was this a lesson for me? Was it a lesson for people who believe that they are in control of when and what happens in their lives?

Then there's a lesson each of us should learn and it should be copyrighted. The game is Dial a Prayer – a game played at great length by preachers, teachers, men and women in various circumstances.

Some those of you who do not know the rules of the game, you may place a call at any time from any location. You will always be connected and will find (a) someone ready to listen, (b) comfort during your moments of frustration, (c) hope for the future. When you hang up you will (a) realize that it's not about you, (b) be ready to face future challenges, and (c) be hopeful about your outcome. However, you must follow the guidelines of the game. Know where your place is on the board at all times and when it's your time to speak and to listen. The game could take minutes, or even hours, but you must know the rules for leaving and returning to the game. I play it often. When I play it right, I am almost always a winner!

At times, there are interruptions in the game that leads to delayed results. As I was sitting there waiting for my stylist a supplier walked in to deliver some new products. I noticed that she had the new curling iron I had be admiring in TV ads for months. Finally it was available in the salon and I could see how it actually works before purchasing one. The young lady delivering the product turned to me and said I looked like someone she knew in Ohio. I took a closer look and much to my surprise it was my daughter's college classmate. She looked at me and yelled, "You are Zina's mom!" Then said five words in excitement: God works in mysterious ways.

Overcome by a somewhat "strange feeling" of astonishment, I examined the reasons why God had allowed me to be delayed from doing what I wanted to do with my time. It turned out that the cosmetic supply girl and my daughter had actually attended college together and members of the same sorority. They had moved to Georgia together and stayed in close contact until she relocated to Alabama. Recapturing their friendship would be a joyous event. I called my daughter up on her cellphone and left the rest to them.

Delays and disruptions regarding our planned activities translate into waiting for God's answer. In fact, my waiting experience paid off in multiple ways. One, I had a well-needed talk with the Lord through a silent prayer. I was able to acquire a product I had wanted for a while. Plus, my hairstyle turned out fabulous. I was allowed to deliver a blessing to my daughter in the form of her friend.

Ways to Wait

Before God moves we will wait. God hears our prayers, however, he does not move when we say. God knows what we need and when we need it. Nobody gets out of waiting, so the question is how do we wait?

David had a secret of waiting and being a man after God's own heart. David went in before the Lord, sat with Him and received guidance from Him. David trusted God, 2 Samuel 7:18. David trusted God for his defense against the enemy and for his strength. He took refuge in God.

Waiting tries our faith but taking matters into our own hands reveals our impatience and lack of trust. Waiting test our submission to God as our authority. Waiting means that we are under the full direction and protection of God. If we run ahead of God we usually run into more complications.

We learn while we wait. We learn about God, we allow Him to reveal Himself to us. We learn about His omniscience and omnipresence. We learn that God's timing is in our favor. Waiting is one of the tools God uses to develop us. Waiting reveals our true motives and allows God to teach us what is best for us. Waiting builds patience. As we learn to wait for smaller things God prepares us to receive greater things.

Through waiting our character is transformed, we know this from the story of Moses who had to wait in the desert for forty years. God gave him a second chance and the opportunity to become a great leader. We will also be transformed by waiting for God to work in us, for us, and through us.

God's Timing

We all want good things to happen in a timely manner in our lives, however, God says when and not us. Many people think that we can just call Him up and something happens. Most of us are trusting in the "Right Now" and not on God's timing. When focused on your own self-fulfillment prophecies, then you are not trusting God.

A Christian walk requires you to lean solely on the Lord for the solution. However, uncomfortable it may be God will never have you to bear more than you are capable of bearing. Trusting God requires not always knowing how He will do something, but trusting that He will. He doesn't speed things up for us; He's never late with His answer. Everything He does is on time.

Perspectives on Waiting

One of the perspectives of waiting is having patience. Patience is a fruit of the spirit (Galatians 5:22). Patience is developed over time and only through trial. Learning to be patient takes practice and will strengthen us. Since patience involves change we know that our relationship with God will change also, for the better.

Acceptance is another perspective of waiting for God. God gives our hopes and dreams to us so that He can carry out His plans for our lives. Our not knowing the timing keeps Him in control and allows us to see His glory. We learn to live in hope and how to experience the joy and peace that comes from living in Him. God knows when we are ready. Just as He lead the Israelites in a longer and harder journey to the Promised Land, we may have to go through some wearisome situations to get to where He wants us.

We must learn to rely on God and not on ourselves. Proverbs 16:9 says, "A person's steps are directed by the Lord. How then can anyone understand their own way?" We must let God direct our path because His way is always the right way. It may not be pleasant and we may not understand it, but when we trust in Him we are saying to Him, "I trust you Lord, and my life is in your hands." Proverbs 3:5, 6 tells us to "Trust in the Lord with all your heart and lean not to your own understanding, in all your ways submit to him, and he will make your paths straight."

Eagerly Waiting

Once we've turned a problem or situation over to God, we need to wait eagerly for His solution. We should be actively serving Him as we wait with the greatest expectation. God loves a heart that is trusting and eager to glorify Him with a sweet spirit of faith. The waiting period often serves as a period of preparation He uses to get us ready to receive His solution.

Occasionally we find ourselves in such disorder during the waiting and cannot imagine what the way out would look like. But what we need to do is keep waiting and trusting because God has already worked it out in Heaven and is just waiting till the time is right to present it to us. Just remember what God said in Jeremiah 29:11, "For I know the plans I have for you," declares the Lord, "plans to prosper you and not to harm you, plans to give you hope and a future."

The Waiting Game

As I learn to wait on the Lord, I do everything that I can to gain a better understanding of his plan for me. Meaning, I study to learn more about Him and I practice communicating with Him so that I will know how to turn my problems and responsibilities over to Him.

A good player must be willing to learn the rules of the game and willing to follow the leader. That means leaving everything up to God and playing the game His way.

Successful gamers study the plays and develop strategies for accomplishing the goals based on the rules. These are the same strategies a great leader uses to conquer his enemy. He watches, waits and delivers success.

The Efforts of Waiting

Four years ago my husband James decided to retire from Ford Motor Company after 40 years of service. I was happy about his decision. We decided to pack up our home, sell it, and move to Atlanta to be near our daughter and her family. The home sold immediately. In fact, it sold in less than 10 days. I was thrilled to be leaving the cold weather in Ohio.

We were scheduled to close on February 20, 2009. But, the buyer was so determined to get into the home earlier that we went ahead and closed on February 6, 2009. I told our realtor on several occasions that we could not leave until after the end of the month. This resulted in us living in a hotel in Cleveland for almost three weeks as we finalized our relocation plans.

I had ignored the plans James had for us and rushed and sold the house. I had to learn quickly how to wait on God because though the home in Ohio sold so quickly, getting to Georgia and purchasing another home was the real test.

We arrived in Atlanta on March 2, 2009. Our appointments with a realtor went poorly. She showed us everything but what we were looking for. Plus, she did everything from take her daughter with her to stopping at a store to purchase something for her husband. James and I were disgusted because we had to move in with our daughter and son-in-law. Anxious to be in our own place we began to search on our own. We later conducted an online search and acquired a new realtor to show us the homes.

For some compelling reason, I was in a hurry to buy a home and what I though was the perfect one was right there for our choosing. I had always dreamed of living in this huge mansion in this beautiful community and here it was in reach and I could have it. The price was right and it wasn't far from our kids. We moved in not considering the size of the home and the labor and upkeep involved with a home this size. Why would two people need six bedrooms and six bathrooms anyway?

I became more convinced that while God does answer prayers. He wants us to be mindful of what we ask for. Because now here we were in this huge home with rooms we would never use and a place so large that lacked the feeling of warmth we wanted in a home. I had prayed and asked God for several things. He let them all happen to teach me a valuable lesson. By the ninth month, we were ready to go and again even with the housing market being so weak. God allowed us to sell the home and purchase another. Unfortunately, the second home in Georgia wasn't what we wanted either. We realized that we moved took quickly and we simply do not like Georgia.

James and I, are now living in Alabama and we are "waiting on the Lord" to reveal to us what His plans are for us. In our daily devotions, we learn and listen to everything He wants us to know. I have decided that waiting on God is the antidote to all of life's ills.

Tired of Waiting

Are you waiting to turn the right age for Social Security? Waiting to retire? Waiting for a buyer for your home? Waiting to find the right house or waiting for a job? Or what about waiting for a lung, a kidney, or liver? Eventually, everyone has to wait for something. As we discussed earlier in this book, many people in the Bible had to wait. We talked about, Abraham and Sarah, Jacob and Rachel, David, Jesus waited to begin His ministry and many others did the same. Just like them, we have to wait.

You may even feel tired and emotionally crippled. But just hold on to your faith. "Wait training" is designed to strengthen your spiritual muscles and get you ready for the marathon of glory. Waiting is a discipline that produces a righteous character and leads to peace for a Christian. Hebrews 12:11, tells us, "No discipline seems pleasant at the time, but painful. Later on, however, it produces a harvest of righteousness and peace for those who have been trained by it" (NIV).

How to Grow Strong as We Wait for God

Waiting for what seems impossible would be a deterrent for anyone. Consider how a dieter feels when he or she decides to go on a weight loss regiment. They know that they have to change something about the way they do things and even the way they eat. They know that when they do a transformation will take place. However, that doesn't make it any easier. It is only through commitment and determination to accomplish their goal that they can survive.

Jesus is the perfect fitness trainer, because He doesn't allow you to cheat. He is in charge of the entire program and you are not getting off easy. The program involves exercising your patience and prayer muscles and wearing your spiritual workout suit because you are going to sweat. The best part about the whole program is He stays with you the entire time. All you have to do is study His word and call on Him. When you feel weak just praise Him. He will strengthen you as you wait.

As any training does, "wait training" requires consistency too. You must be consistent in spending time with God in prayer and in service to build your spiritual endurance. The more you know the more you grow. Study His word as you wait and prepare yourself for *joy* that He has promised those who trust Him. Stay calm and know that God is always in control. In 1 Corinthian 10:3, it states, "Whether you eat or drink or whatever you do, do it all for the glory of God."

Glorify God as We Wait

Our chief purpose is to glorify God and to enjoy Him throughout eternity. It is God who gave us our being and to Him be the glory. Romans 11:36, tells us that "For Him, and through Him, are all things." In glorifying God, we must show Him the highest appreciation. Glorifying Him consists of adoring Him, trusting Him, and worshiping Him. Psalm 29:2 said, "Give unto the Lord the glory due unto His name; worship the Lord in the beauty of holiness."

To glorify God is to acknowledge the essence of His nature and greatness. We must give God honor by praising and worshiping Him. Glorifying God is accepting and agreeing with everything He said about Himself that includes waiting. God declares who He is in Isaiah, "Thus says God, the Lord, who created the heavens and stretched them out, who spread out the earth and what comes from it, who gives breath to the people on it and spirit to those who walk in it." We must praise Him because of who He is. We must give Him the Glory and honor that He so deserves.

In glorifying Him, we must also show Him affection by loving Him as Deuteronomy 6:5 says, "Thou shalt love the Lord thy God with all thy heart and with all thy soul." We must glorify Him by being subjective to Him. Subjection requires us to dedicate ourselves to serving Him and His people everywhere. God is love and all hope hangs upon Him.

Chapter 8

Breaker, Breaker:
God Wants Your Attention

"Breaker, breaker one nine", "Go ahead Johnny B. Good", "What's your twenty?" The answer may have been, "At your back door" or, "How is it looking over your shoulder?" The response would be, "Clean and green so you can put the pedal to the medal for now." Then you might hear "Ten four good buddy, it's looking pretty good your way too." When I first met my husband he was heavily involved with CB radios. I remember, taking trips with him and having to listen to him and his CB friends known as "good buddies" for hours on end.

At that time, monitoring traffic, retrieving information related to state troopers about location and accidents, and just having "a friend on the road" to communicate with for directions or to call for emergency help was the thing. Unlike today, where there are GPS systems and the extensive use of smartphones.

The government has developed stringent safeguards surrounding all forms of communications, telecommunications, and technology has become the driving factor in industry and distribution of information. Today, wireless technologies use radio waves to transmit light, magnetic, and electric fields for short and long-range communications that power use of transmitters, receivers, remote controls and other devices. Communications are monitored and regulated by the Federal Communications Commission system (FCC). The FCC regulates interstate and international radio, television, satellite and cable communications. It was through the use of our newly purchased cellphone in 1999 that, James and I received the message to turn around from our trip back to Ohio because his father had passed away from cancer following our visit. This was no CD radio transmission or FCC test.

The road from Hartselle, Alabama, to Cumberland, Kentucky, wasn't one we were accustomed to traveling. The cellphone and radio reception between the Tennessee and Kentucky mountains was very limited. However, just as we reached the Kentucky state line our cellphone rang a call from my mother-in-law informed us that his dad had passed away. For a few moments, everything got quiet. I could see the sadness on my husband's face. I offered to drive the remainder of the trip but he wouldn't have it. I believe concentrating on the road helped him take his mind off of the pain.

After a long period of silence, James shouted out the most common curse word "damn". My first thought was, "He is upset that we will have to turn around and drive straight back to Alabama, or was he mad at God?" People say things like that in "the face of disappointment" about their favorite team losing, their car stalling, when running late, or facing great tragedy. In this case, it was the heartbreaking death of his father. Life just isn't fair and God could have timed things a little differently, but He didn't.

Things "as they are" vs. "how they ought to be" represent the perpetual strain between what is taking place and what we think should happen. Is God unfair? Shouldn't God have allowed James's father to pass away while he was there? What are the rules? Was God using Dad's death to punish Him? A Scripture came to my mind, "All the trees of the field will know that I the LORD bring down the tall tree and make the low tree grow tall. I dry up the green tree and make the dry tree flourish. I the Lord have spoken, and I will do it" (Ezekiel 17:24). God apparently wanted to teach James something and was giving him time to think.

The suffering took over his thoughts. "Why would God put me through all of this?" James asked. He is after all is a good and loving son who cared deeply for his father and had spent many precious hours with him before he died. "Look at me," James said "I am the only one of his children who has forgiven him for divorcing our mother and leaving us to marry his best friend's wife. I even forgave her and I cared for both of them." He went on and on as we drove through Kentucky, talking about what he had done for his father. As I thought about it, I began to wonder if he had really forgiven his father or was he upset that dad had died before he could tell him how he felt. "Was he angry at God or himself?"

Attacks of the Enemy

Death and other unforeseen situations sometimes cause us to question God. Why would God put man in stressful situations? Such "a notion" calls for a question that every believer should ask themselves, "What does God want me to learn?" Many people look at situations that happen to them as unfairness. Attacks come in many forms and can produce hopelessness and despair in the lives of Christians.

Entering Cumberland, Kentucky later that evening was the best thing that could have happened to us. We shared the information about his grief with my family. Fortunately, it was late so everyone talked for a few minutes and went to bed. The next day, James and I, headed out for our return trip to Alabama. My sweet little mother prayed with us and whispered to James, "God's got it all in control." A gentle calm came over us. The entire drive to Alabama was pleasant.

James was able to talk about his father and reminisced about many joyful memories from his childhood. Later, he reflected on several traumatic events he had blotted out of his memory for so long. And though he discussed them very little over the years, I could tell by his reactions that they made him feel helpless. This is what was really troubling him.

After admitting to some mean things his father did to his mother and to him as a child, James realized that he had never truly released himself from the bondage of the past. He had spent time with his father but never really discussed what he had been feeling all those years. It was too late now. But don't blame God when you fail to do your part. Satan had been attacking him through his thoughts. As we continued to talk, I began praying. He replied, "I am not sure of what just happened but talking with God helped me to see things a little clearer. Dad is gone now and I can't punish him for something he wasn't even aware of. I have to cherish his memory."

It was good to pray and talk about his father. When we arrived to Alabama "all hell" had broken loose. Numerous relatives had arrived from Ohio and other locations upset to learn that their father would not be buried in the traditional Baptist way. He had joined another denomination and the funeral would be based on his beliefs. We knew that his father wasn't of the same faith and that he would have a special funeral service; however his family members didn't know and were quite troubled by it.

Thank God, He had been dealing with my husband's heart in advance. I knew there must be a reason God allowed us to leave Alabama when we did. I am almost sure it was so that he could recondition my husband's heart and allow him to calmly cooperate with the burial plans our mother-in-law had made for his father. We almost had a boxing match at the funeral! But James and I remembered what the Bible said about forgiveness:

> Bearing with one another and, if one has a complaint against another, forgiving each other; as the Lord has forgiven you, so you also must forgive" (Colossians 3:13, ESV).

Attacks produce hopelessness and gloom in the lives of Christians and non-Christians. Attacks may be launched by human enemies who are filled with self-indulgence, guilt, or anger.

My husband's family was holding on to past angry related to the divorce and marriage, and the religion issues only made things worse. Though I didn't believe this was a time to act ugly, Satan is the author of confusion. Why couldn't they just let their loved one be put away in peace?

Satan is often the motivator of attacks on mankind. Our defense against such attacks is to put on the full armor of God. Ephesians 6:11 states, "Put on the full armor of God, so that you can take your stand against the devil's schemes." Being armed during despair strengthens your hope. We made it through that horrible ordeal and on the way back I reflected on my earlier years when I first learned how Satan attacks.

While in my youth growing up in the mountains of Kentucky, walking up a dark road was nothing to some people. They would laugh, skip, and play just as much as they did during the daytime. At

Christmas, Halloween, Fourth of July, and especially Memorial Day, people were out until the wee hours of the morning.

These traditions provided the people of Eastern Kentucky with joyful memories of fun and entertainment. While most were entertained, I was scared senseless over what I may step on or what may come from under a Halloween mask or at other times grab me from the woods.

All I could think about were those Bible stories about Satan and what I had heard about wickedness and evil spirits. The book of Revelations had put the fear of God in me. Especially, Revelation 12:9, "And the great dragon was cast out, that old serpent, called the Devil, and Satan, which deceiveth the whole world: he was cast out into the earth, and his angels were cast out with him."

My purpose for discussing Satan and demons is not to expound on the topic but to point to the real cause for most of man's problems. It is also impossible to discuss hope without identifying the causes for hopelessness and fear. We must learn not to fear. Satan brings fear as an approach to ruling God's people and to keep them from coming under submission to the true Master, Jesus. I encourage all Christians to take self-inventory and don't be afraid to forgive others. Jesus said in Isaiah 41:10, to fear not because He is with us. So go forward with God in love and in peace.

No One is Exempt

Several years ago, my husband and I were privileged to own a travel business and go to numerous places around the world. In 1998, we decided to travel to Brazil to attend Carnival. The Olympics were taking place in Brazil at that time, making the trip that much more exciting. We traveled to numerous sites in Brazil and visited the Corcovado and Sugarloaf Mountains. The Corcovado is an iconic Christ the Redeemer statue overlooking Rio de Janerio on the mountain called Pinaculo da Tentacao, which translates to Pinnacle of Temptation.

More than 360 people travel up and down this 2,300 feet high mountain every hour to view the statue with its outstretched arms. Once on the top many visitors take advantage of the souvenir shop, the chapel, the beaches, the ocean, and the surrounding mountains. However, a vast majority of visitors seek to have some spiritual connection with the statue.

The original statue was designed in 1921, by Carlos Oswaldo and was carrying a cross. However, the sculptor was changed by engineer Paul Landowsi omitting the cross. The Catholic Church inaugurated the statue in October, 1931. "Here we stood, I cannot believe… Watching hundreds of people walk up to a statue built in 1921, believing that they would receive some kind of power. Lord have mercy on your people."

The second most memorable and captivating scenery was that of visiting several neighborhoods in Rio de Janeiro. We hired a driver one day. Our destination was to see where and how the people lived in Brazil. We remembered on our descent into Brazil seeing homes that appeared to have no roofs. As the driver took us into the city we spotted what appeared to be the area we had observed from the airplane. At the top of a hill just past the beach and resort area where we were staying stood what appeared to be a town in total devastation. My heart quivered when the driver said to us this is where many of the people of Rio live.

We were shown streets with multiple apartments and broken down houses. The streets filled with garbage, and the buildings were without doors or roofs. We saw dead animal carcasses all over and people would walk up to the cars begging for food. Pregnant women were walking in the streets naked. Located about two miles away at the bottom of the hill was an outside market where people sold everything you could imagine. The driver had warned us ahead of time not to wear jewelry or dress fancy because crime was high in that area. We adhered to what he said and let all jewelry at our resort and wore comfortable clothing. Yet it was not enough to distract onlookers and beggars.

The driver told us that Brazilian people are usually affectionate but to avoid giving them any gifts that is black or purple because they are perceived as mourning colors. Though the majority of the people were Catholic, African migrants and other immigrants had brought different religious influences making it a very complex culture. With that I can understand why so many of Brazil's people rush to worship a statue.

We learned from an online magazine article *Countries and Their Cultures* that Brazil is the largest Catholic country in the world. The Catholic Church population in Brazil has declined from the 95 percent that existed in the 1950s to 73% today (Every culture, 2014). Nonetheless, *Candomblé* is the best known and most traditional religion in many areas of Brazil followed by Umbanda another highly spiritual religion. These spiritualistic beliefs grew out of African and French followers and are viewed by many in Brazilian Catholicism as the work of the Devil. Though we did not physically see the Devil, we saw signs of depression and chaos suggesting he was at work.

Satan and Martin Luther

In the early Sixteenth-century many European theologians and scholars began questioning the teachings of the Roman Catholic Church. It was around this time, the Bible and other writings in the early church were translated into original text for German Augustinian monasteries. Augustine (340-430) had emphasized the priority of the Bible as the ultimate religious authority rather than the church. He believed that humans were incapable of reaching salvation on their own, and that God alone could bestow salvation by His divine grace. The Catholic Church taught that salvation was possible through "good work". Martin Luther, (1483) was and came to share Augustine's two beliefs and would later rebel against Catholicism forming the basis of Protestantism.

Martin Luther was critical of the Catholic Church and his central teachings were that the Bible is the central source of religious authority and that salvation is reached only through faith. As a result of his beliefs, Luther wrote the "Disputation on the Power and Efficacy of Indulgences," also known as "The 95 Theses" which became the foundation for the Protestant reformation.

Satan's Complete Purpose

This information is shared with you to inform you that humans everywhere are susceptible to battles with satanic oppression and despair. The attacks on both believers and non-believers are consistent with Satan's purpose. As explained Satan is a liar by nature. He lies about who God is, about us, and about God's plans for us. Satan is constantly seeking ways to harm Christians and the world through brainwashing people of the world to accept false philosophies. Scripture tells us, "We know that we are children of God, and that the whole world is under the control of the evil one" (1 John 5:19). We are told in John 8:44 that Satan is the father of lies.

Satan hates Jesus, the Heavenly Father, and the Holy Spirit. Therefore, every person that has been born is in danger of his traps. Paul's says in Ephesians 6:11 that Christians must put on the full armor of God against the devil's schemes. We are warned in Matthew 6:9-15 of Satan's attempts to hold us captive to unforgiving spirits. God wants us to acknowledge our faults and the faults of our offenders and forgive them.

Satan's Strategies

How does Satan "steal our joy and destroy or hope"? Satan fears those who love Jesus Christ so he exposes them to ultimate pain, sorrow, death, and despair. He tries to discourage us from doing anything that pleases God. No one is safe from Satan and he would rather have us miserable throughout our lifetime than see us serving God. But God's plan is better.

God's plan is to grant us peace, joy, and eternal life. All He requires from us is that we seek Him in prayer. He will guide us the rest of the way to the wisdom and understanding of His Word. Jesus will hear our prayers and He will answer them according to His will for what is best for us.

One of Satan's key strategies is blinding believer's minds through deception. This is Satan's most successful tool because it keeps an individual from seeing clearly.

Satan's Attack on the Family

In the Bible, God makes it clear that we are engaged in a spiritual warfare with Satan. In Ephesians 6:10-18, we are advised to put on the full armor of God. Peter describes Satan as our adversary who "prowls around like a roaring lion seeking someone to devour" (Peter 5:8 NIV). In Genesis 3:1 NIV, Satan is described as the serpent "more crafty than any of the wild animals the Lord God had made." Satan is a deceiver," (John 8:44-45 NIV). "He was a murderer from the beginning, not holding to the truth, for there is no truth in him." Paul calls him the "god of this world who has blinded the minds of unbelievers, to keep them from seeing the light of the glory of Christ" (2 Cor. 4:4). Satan seeks to prevent people from receiving the blessings God has for them by devising evil tricks to turn them against God.

The devil knows that marriage and family are sacred and represents Christ and the church. Marriage and family were designed for the good of mankind. Satan knows that family is the foundation of a strong society. He also knows that a strong society is the foundation for carrying out the work of God. Satan aims to break every stronghold he can by destroying God's property, the family.

Satan's Attack on the Institution of Marriage

God called his creation of the first man and woman "good." God created them with the purpose of benefiting future generations. He did not want man to be alone and for that reason a holy bond was created. The Lord also had guidelines regarding marriage. He explained, "Therefore a man shall leave his father and his mother and hold fast to his wife, and they shall become one flesh" (Genesis 2:24, ESV). In marriage God requires a commitment between the man and woman which will provide a foundation for the family unit they create.

The old serpent, Satan initially attacked the family in the Garden of Eden by deceiving Eve and destroying the family unity. Eve disobeyed God thus bringing a curse of all future families. Satan's attack continue today in the number of divorces, common law marriages, polygamy, legalization of same gender marriages, and marriages of children and adults for profit. Through a twisted society we are being deprived of Christian unity and having what God intends to be the best for married people.

Satan's Internal Attack on the Family

A good marriage is the foundation of a good family. When Satan has the opportunity to destroy a marriage the family has no other course but to crumble. When marriages crumble, the children begin to react by displaying behavioral disorders that normally would not exist. Behavior disorders are exhibited by 85% of the children from fatherless homes according to *Statistics on Fatherless Children in America* (Parker, 2014). Sixty-three percent of the suicides among children in America are by children from fatherless homes. The Scriptures provide guidelines for the entire family.

Satan's Motive in Attacking the Christian Home

Satan knows that within the home of a strong married couple the word of God is taught and practiced. The Godly life is if exemplified from generation to generation. An example is the life of faith Timothy displayed. Attitudes of faith were demonstrated from the grandmother of Timothy to his own life. From his youth, he was acquainted with the Holy Scriptures which made him wise about salvation through faith in Jesus Christ" (2 Tim 3:15-17).

Parents have the responsibility of introducing the word of God to their children and maintaining a constant flow of Bible knowledge and prayer in their homes. Children learn by example when they see the importance of having God in their lives. Solomon advises parents to, "Train up a child in the way he should go, and when he is old he will not turn from it" (Proverb 22:6, ESV). Families who recognize God's plan for them and live accordingly are glorifying Him by being obedient and living as He commands us to.

Parents who live Godly lives in the presence of their children demonstrate the word of God and provide guidance for their children. When Satan can prevent parents from exhibiting Christian attributes such as the "Fruits of the Spirit" (Galatians 5:22-23) love, joy, peace, patience, kindness, goodness, faithfulness gentleness, and self-control he accomplishes his goal of diminishing God's truth. The family's safety lay in knowing God's word and live by His commandments.

Furthermore, it is God who created the family, and He did provide instructions in His Word for families to live by. By becoming competent in His Word and practicing the fruits of the spirit family can distinguish between right and wrong choices and find safety against Satan's assaults.

Satan's Attack on the Church

Satan doesn't only attack married people and their family. He has launched a full fledge attack on the church. In a recent online magazine article entitled *7 Ways Satan Attacks the Church,* author Ron Edmondson referred to Peter by describing what Satan is doing to people in and out of the church. "Your adversary the Devil is prowling around like a roaring lion, looking for anyone he can devour." (1 Peter 5:8). Satan loves disrupting the harmony of the church especially since he knows that he is limited. Jesus confirmed who He was when He spoke to Simon Peter saying:

> *Blessed are you, Simon Bar-Jonah! For flesh and blood has not revealed this to you, but my Father who is in heaven. And I tell you, you are Peter, and on this rock I will build my church, and the gates of hell shall not prevail against it. I will give you the keys of the kingdom of heaven, and whatever you bind on earth shall be bound in heaven, and whatever you loose on earth shall be loosed in heaven."* (Matthew 16:17-19, ESV)

The seven ways in which Satan tries to destroy the church are through burnout, rumors, busyness, lies, scandal, marriage and family disruptions (Edmondson, 2014). The seven ways in which he attacks are: (1) He forces church leaders and officers to become burnt out and he can make them feel unappreciated, (2) Satan plants the seed of disruption by stirs strife through the spread of rumors about members of the church or the community, (3) through the use of scandals Satan divides churches, separates people and destroys members ability to effectively accomplish work for the Kingdom, (4) Satan devises ways to lure individuals into becoming preoccupied with other events therefore making them too busy for church, (5) Satan attempts to interject false doctrine into the body of Christ causing skepticism and separation within the church, (6) Satan to use gossip to split, and divide the church body, and (7) By destroying marriages and homes Satan strengthens his attack against the church.

Fortunately, there is a remedy for attacks by Satan the destroyer. His name is Jesus Christ. God wants us to know that, "You, dear children, are from God and have overcome them, because the one who is in you is greater than the one who is in the world." (1 John 4:4, NIV) He is also aware of every weapon Satan uses against us.

Satan discourages us from searching God's Word and whispers to our spirits to neglect praying to God. He knows that if we pray and study God's word we will receive God's power and the truths that God wants us to know will be revealed. God's plan is for us to strengthen our faith and knowledge of Him.

Satan wants us to believe that the Bible doesn't apply to us today. He wants to trick us as he did Job by getting us to believe that God doesn't care about us. But God's promise to us is, "Blessed is he who reads and those who hears the words of this prophecy, and keep those things which are written in it" (Revelation 1:3, NKJV). The Lord wants us to know how to be saved.

The things we fear most on this earth, such as violence, terrorism, and unbelievers and far from being our greatest threats. The greatest threat to mankind is the danger of ignoring God. "How shall we escape if we neglect so great salvation?" (Hebrew 2:3, NIV). We must avoid being spiritually anorexic. Spiritual anorexia is like depriving ourselves of the well needed nutrition required to clean and purify us.

Just as a person with and eating disorder is affected mentally, physically, and emotionally, a person with spiritual anorexia becomes susceptible to mental, emotional, and physical losses. Once this takes place an individual's self-identity insights, an ability to cope is threatened. This is why Satan doesn't want us to be feed by the Word of God. But our "Best Friend" is Jesus and He is always near if we call on Him.

Satan says we are unimportant to God and if we have a problem we should consult him. But Isaiah tells us, "When men tell you to consult mediums and spirits, who whisper and mutter, should not a people inquire of their God? Why consult the dead on behalf of the living?" (Isaiah 8:19-20). And Christ does claim, "I am the way and the truth and the Life, No one comes to the Father except through me." (John 14:6). Many of God's children have been deceived by Satan who wants them to believe that the storms they face are because God doesn't care. It is quite the opposite. God proved His love for us through sacrificing His son Jesus.

Two of the most wonderful people I know and I have talked about in this book!

Mrs. Pitts *Evangelist Dorthy Culbreth*

Chapter 9

Destined to Survive

I grew up in Eastern Kentucky, the fourth of five children. You read earlier chapters about some of the events that have taken place in my life. However, there were some good memorable times in the Quarles household too. Family commencing together every Sunday for supper around 1:30 p.m. for a delicious meal. Come to think of it, those were the best times I had with my family. Except an occasional visit my favorite uncle George from Ohio would come home on Memorial Day to visit and shower everyone with presents. The year of my graduation I was ready to go back with him.

The Sabbath was sacred to both of my maternal grandparents but church was not always the place my uncle wanted to visit when he came home. One particular weekend, we children were so fascinated by the "city man in the big car" that all of us children wanted to do nothing more than snuggle up under him and my aunt Norma and open our gifts. Dinner that day took second place. My grandmother didn't like my uncle's wife very much. Many times, they stayed with other relatives to avoid arguments in the household.

As children, we couldn't make the decision about where our uncle stayed because no one overruled my grandmother. It was a Memorial Weekend and I knew that we would be leaving Kentucky headed to Cleveland on Monday morning. I was excited and not too concerned about the other things going on around me. I spent the weekend packing my bags ready to go.

Memorial Day was celebrated on Monday, May 20, 1968 and so was my departure from Kentucky. I said goodbye to beatings, name calling, heartache and pain and to everything that made me sad. The only hurt I felt was leaving my beautiful mother. I knew that I would see her again. I wasn't too concerned about my sweet little sister Andrea who was the only child left at home now. She was the love of my mom's life and was always treated special. I knew that no harm would come to her either.

As we got in the car to drive away, my grandfather walked over and prayed with us. I will never forget him kissing me on the cheek and saying, "Now go and be happy." It was like he could see into my future or something.

The next day, we arrived in Cleveland and spent the first few days unpacking and getting familiarized with the house rules and the neighborhood. A few days later, my aunt and uncle drove me into the city and introduced me to friends and relatives I had never met. I was fascinated by the lights, the highways, and the tall buildings. "Wow!" I thought, "I have died and gone to heaven." Everything was so different from the hills and mountains I was accustomed to and the houses were even larger and prettier. At home I brought up the topic of religion, but there wasn't much discussion-other than my aunt was not of the same faith and does not attend the same type of church I was accustomed to. I thought, "This must be the reason my grandmother doesn't like her."

What are you Praying for?

You pray long and hard for something and then it happens. Okay what's next? I learned soon after moving with my aunt and uncle that adults in real life just don't behave like they do on television. My aunt and uncle were both very kind to me but had a strange way of showing love for each other. That was called "grown folks business" and I knew to stay out of it. Anyway, I knew from all the times I had been around Uncle George and Aunt Norma that even though they had a funny way of showing it they loved each other. I just didn't understand how they were kinder to other people than to each other.

At the time I moved to Ohio, my aunt and uncle only had the one child and he meant the world to his parents. I loved being with them and taking care of my little cousin. That first year seemed to pass by so quickly. So much happened in a year. I had gotten a part-time job and enrolled in college. My world was moving so fast. Before I knew it I was in love with a handsome young man who worked for the same company as my uncle. A year later we were married.

He was my knight in shining armor for five years. Ironically he began to show me another side of himself and became my nightmare. We had a nice home to live in, nice furniture, and three beautiful little babies. Reality had not set in until one day a lady called to inform me that she was his girlfriend and was expecting his child. Of course, he denied everything several times but eventually I discovered that it was true. I was crushed. My blessed and fruitful life was in shambles.

I was determined to survive so I packed up my babies and our clothes and went home to my mother. I already had in mind what I wanted to do with the rest of my life. I prayed to the Lord and I said to the devil, "I may be broken, but I am not defeated." I stayed with my mother for a couple of months but God allowed me to be accepted at the University of Louisville where I attended for the next two years. God had blessed me again by allowing "My Little Buddies" and me to get settled into a nice new home. I was so thankful that we did not have to be apart for any long period of time.

My prayers fell on the ears of God and He heard my cries. My children and I settled in Louisville, Kentucky in an apartment near the University of Louisville campus and found a nice church to attend. When friends and church members heard I was a single parent and a college student, they thought that was extraordinary and made extra efforts to assist us. I was truly grateful to the kind people who aided me during these times. I still communicate with many of them.

I sometimes felt like the biggest hypocrite in the world because the people were doing so much for me and I was too busy to put in quality time in church activities. "No, no, you will get your chance," Mrs. Ragglin, one of my favorite elderly friends in the church would say to me, "During the first three years all I did was study and work. But I woke up one morning and realized that I had time on my hands. My children and I got super busy in the church and the community."

I worked a couple of years in Louisville for Jefferson County Department of Human Services and in 1981 received a job offer from Allen Count Children Services Board in Lima, Ohio which was too good to turn down. The children and I relocated to Lima where we stayed for three years. Bye-bye First Baptist Church of Louisville. We spent three precious years in Lima. This was a learning experience for me and the children. We purchased a home in a place called Elida, Ohio, which was out in the country and all we really had there was each other. After being so bored with nothing to do and longing to be around other people we decided to move back to Cleveland.

This time it would be different. I wasn't running away from my grandmother or my ex-husband. God had given me a second chance. I was offered a well-paying job by Prudential Insurance Company where I served as a Financial Advisor for three years. I was the youngest and most productive worker in my office. I received several outstanding sales certificates and from Life Underwriters Training Council (LUTC) and other organizations affiliated with the insurance industry. When I could no longer stand the flirting by the male staff or the jealousy of competitive co-workers I knew it was time to go back to college and move on. I met some very influential people who had a great impact on my life. But when God says go, you go.

The next few years were humbling because not only did I meet my husband who I've been married to for over 33 years, I met friends who richly enhanced my life. Until I met my husband I had not known anyone who cared so deeply about the salvation of people who were incarcerated. James was and still is deeply involved in prison ministry and witnessing to the unsaved.

I had put my foot in my mouth and stepped out on faith. I remember reading in a book by Ellie Lofaro titled *Leap of Faith,* "Where foot-in-mouth syndrome abounds, grace abounds all the more." Cleveland Councilman Tyrone Bolden and his wonderful wife, Lucretia became a bright light for me. They embraced me with a Godly love put their arms around me. Tyrone is the Pastor of a well-known church in Cleveland and Lucretia is one of the best gospel singers I have ever heard. I was so impressed by the way they helped people in the Cleveland communities and how they both reached out to help young black men and women complete their college education.

I went to work at Cleveland City Council in 1989 as administrative assistant to Councilman Bolden. There was never a day that he, his wife or her family didn't acknowledge the presence of God in their lives. Their love for God's people and for the community gave me a sincere respect for who they are in Christ. I have looked up to them ever since and always acknowledge them in my prayers of gratitude. After I moved back to Cleveland and met these wonderful people I realized that home was wherever Jesus is.

As life passes by and you wait patiently on God, it is a good time to examine yourself to see who you are in Christ. Though the things that happened yesterday had an impact on the choices you make, remember, yesterday is gone and God gives us new mercies each day. On the other hand, though the first few years of my life were stressful, today is the beginning of the rest of my life. That goes for everyone. Second Corinthians 5:17 tells us, "Therefore, if anyone is in Christ, the new creation has come: The old has gone, the new is here!"

Recognizing when Prayers are Answered

Prayer is that essential part of our relationship with God that keeps us connected to Him. However, many times we do not recognize when our prayers have been answered. We are often so caught up in a whirlpool of human emotions that we fail to see what God has done for us.

It is wrong to assume that God is putting us on hold or has forgotten about us. The Lord put us on this earth to succeed. Sometimes He answers and sometimes He doesn't. When He answers us it is for our good and when He doesn't answer it is also for our good. God is aware of our every need and always provides the right answer. His purpose for us is to gain eternal joy and for that reason He encourages us to be mindful of the choices we make.

Perhaps my experiences in the past were allowed to teach me how to pray and how to recognize when He answers my prayer. In any event, I learned that God speaks to our hearts. Many people seek answers for the solution to getting their prayers answered without going to the right source. Jesus says in the Scripture, "If you remain in me and my words remain in you, ask whatever you wish, and it will be given you" (John 15:7). Noticed He used the word *if* to let you know that His promises are conditional and He used the word *will* meaning He guarantees to deliver on His word. God's Word must abide on the inside of you to receive an answer to your prayer.

You may wonder why God puts certain people in our lives. That question was answered for me by the individuals I have talked about and stories I told throughout this book. The truth is no matter how uncomfortable or incompatible we are to some people or even how we try to avoid certain types of people. Jesus made this statement to His followers in Matthew, "But I say to you, love your enemies, bless them that curse you, do good to them that hate you, and pray for them which despitefully use you, and persecute you."(Matthew 5:44) God wants us to learn from those experiences become mature Christians. He does not want us to be enslaved by disobedience, malice or hatred as mentioned in Titus 3:3.

I am sure that many young people have grown up in dysfunctional environments and want to leave home as I did to escape anger, abuse, fear, and insecurity. However those hurtful relationships helped me to become a better person and a more loving person and I chose to present something different to my children. I also gained a wealth of knowledge from the many friends I met along the way that I can use or reject. You know that your prayers are answered when God expands His vision of love to you.

Our Legacy of Love

As Christians we should be concerned about the people in our lives. No just our family or our friends, but about the church and the community. As we grow in our knowledge and understanding of God we learn that it not just about us. Loving other people as a Christian doesn't mean romantically, but the human love the Bible talks about is like the love Jesus has for all people.

> *"Love our enemies, do good to them, and lend to them without expecting to get anything back. Then your reward will be great, and you will be children of the most High, because He is kind to the grateful and wicked" (Luke 6:35).*

God's love is a gift to us, and He wants us to be an extension of Him. By releasing the love. He has given you to others you are serving as an extension of His light. Loving some people may be challenging and you may need to seek help from the Holy Spirit. Ask the Holy Spirit to help you grow in love toward God and toward others.

The Lives We Touch

I hope that you are beginning to see by now what the relationships with other people in our lives mean. Our legacy of love is more than just our families or our children. We each have a responsibility to God to love the people of the world and all of His creation. I could join a thousand organizations, and write a million books but if someone doesn't read them or someone's life doesn't get transformed by them I have left nothing. I may be the only Christian someone ever meets and the only opportunity to see Christ. The Lord desires to have us be a part of His salvation story.

We may resemble many people, famous and not so famous; however, the only person we should aspire to look and act like is Jesus. We should be working hard to adopt His attributes to show to others the compassion He shows to us. First John 2:6 said, "Whoever says he abides in Him ought to walk in the same way in which He walked." The apostles cautioned us in Colossians 3: 9-10, to put on the new self and not to lie one another, since we are to be renewed in the image of God.

The way to truly leave a Christian legacy is to fear God and be obedient to His Word. Your legacy begins in your heart and in the relationship you have with God. You must know the needs of the world and show compassion for God's people by praying for them and helping them. You must also use your gifts and abilities to serve others.

There is something special about God's people. You may have experienced seeing a person in the grocery line or just in passing at the mall and knew immediately that he or she was a Christian. The Bible said that believers are set apart. God said in Jeremiah 1:5, "Before I formed you in the womb I knew you, before you were born I set you apart; I appointed you as a prophet to the nations. God's love is highly contagious and it attracts people. As a Christian you carry those same traits.

Passing on a Legacy of Faith

A legacy of faith is a spiritual legacy that may not only impact your family but the world. People that come to mind when you think of spiritual legacies are Mother Teresa, Billy Graham, and Dr. Martin Luther King. Many other people have left legacies, some good and some bad. These people left an impact on the lives of people who either met them or heard their stories. A spiritual legacy highlights your relationship with God.

A spiritual legacy is the passing on to the next generation gifts of eternal value that is far more important than any temporal inheritance. Proverbs 13:22 tells us, "A good person leaves an inheritance for their children's children, but a sinner's wealth is stored up for the righteous" (NIV). Our highest priority should be serving God and His people. Pastors and other Christian leaders are responsible for training the children of God. In I Timothy the Word of God says: "For physical training is of some value, but godliness has value for all things, holding promise for both the present life and the life to come" (I Timothy 4:8, NIV).

Godly living has an impact on the people we meet. Hearts change, people listen, and souls are saved when we walk in the light of Jesus Christ. Living a godly life means living with purpose. Our light that shines on earth will also illuminate in heaven. Isaiah 40:8 confirms that God's Word stands forever. If you desire to leave a "spiritual legacy" starts by touching lives of others today.

Chapter 10

Walking by Faith

As long as we can breathe, we can hope. I thought when I was divorced from my first husband that I was a complete failure and I must have done something wrong. I thought the skies of Cleveland, Ohio, were the gloomiest sceneries of my adult life, but my church experience in Canton, Georgia, became the epitome of gloom.

While there is breath there is life, there is hope. But I couldn't see it in my future at the time. Our move to Canton, Georgia, was an experience of a lifetime. There were days I felt like God had dropped me off at the end of the earth. However, I knew He had a purpose for allowing us to move there. Near the end of our stay in Canton, I discovered that God placed me there to "condition my heart" for doing His work aids His children in deep need of spiritual guidance.

I began preparing to move from Canton, Georgia, to a quaint little city just outside of Birmingham, Alabama, called Hoover. It was early February and I was looking forward to seeing my daughter, son-in-law, and grandkids that relocated there a month earlier. A special part of my week also consisted of setting aside to spend with my dear friend Dorothy, my sister in Christ and co-worker in the gospel.

I didn't want to go back to the cold weather in Ohio or back to the city of Atlanta, Georgia. However, Hoover was where my first born and sweet angel girl was moving to. I knew she would miss me as much as I would miss her and the grandchildren. I also needed to see my grandchildren and know that they were okay with their "Honey" nearby.

Dorothy's "angelic spirit" reminded me of my favorite Aunt Mavis who always looked after me as a child. Dorothy was my "Sister Theresa" instead of Mother Theresa – sharing the same attitude about God. Dorothy never had anything negative to say about other people or interested in gossip. Her conversations were always about spiritual things. Not only that, she was ready to pray for others regardless of their physical, mental or emotional conditions.

Dorothy had taken a special interest in me and James from the moment we arrived at the church we attended in Canton, GA. She often did altar call prayers that sounded as if God had whispered in her ears the needs and concerns of those present. She was an excellent minister and loved reading, singing, and teaching the children of the church about God. Not surprisingly, she presented the books of the Bible from perspective that allowed children and adults to gain a clearer understanding of The Word. Sunday mornings were a treat for everyone in attendance.

Although Dorothy was interested in teaching the children about Christ, she was strongly concerned about helping the adults of the church build better relationships with one another and the community. Several months earlier, Dorothy and I, started praying daily for our families, church, and communities. She was involved with several ministries. And, she was especially fond of a ministry her who family served in. Dorothy was very active in a notable women's organization also.

As our car crossed the Georgia line into the state of Alabama, I could see the roads narrowing and an end coming to the six and eight-lane highways, I disliked so much. The familiar Atlanta, Georgia scenery of high rises and city lights was now replaced with two-lane highways and trees. I had left the big city of Cleveland for Georgia where I served as associate pastor and preached many sermons. God only knew where I would go from here. All I knew for sure was my work in Georgia was done.

A Strong Christian Believes

Less than a year later, James and I returned to Atlanta to spend Thanksgiving with close friends we met while living in Georgia. One had just underwent a serious medical challenge and recovered with God's grace. We were aware of our friend's spiritual interest in Christ and amazed at the display of faith the entire family had. There was no way we could travel to Atlanta and not visit our devout Christian friends. Dorothy had impacted our lives in the same special way.

Dorothy had been in the hospital with pneumonia for a few weeks before our visit. We exchanged a few words the morning we hit the road. Dorothy was still a little weak so the visit was top priority.

The day after our arrival, we attended a wedding with friends. And, decided to forgo the reception to spend some quality time with Dorothy. When we arrived at her home, she was sitting in her favorite oversized chair, hooked to oxygen and various tubes. I couldn't imagine what she must have undergone the last few weeks. She was "a picture of hope" for anyone wondering what it means to be a Christian. She had gone through so much in the last six months from losing her mother, losing a great aunt, caring for a sick friend, and watching her church go through chaos and yet she had a huge smile on her face. What could I say about a woman like that?

The Difference Faith Makes

It was not surprising when Dorothy's mother passed away that she would be the main source of support for her family. She helped to facilitate a celebration of life instead of a funeral filed with grief. In fact she got joy out of singing her mother's favorite song during the ceremony.

That is the difference a true Christian makes. It was that belief in eternal life and that blessed assurance that comes with hoping and trusting in Jesus Christ. Dorothy believed like the following verse: "If the Spirit of him who raised Jesus from the dead is living in you, he who raised Christ from the dead will give life to your mortal bodies through his Spirit, who lives in you" (Rom. 8:11). It was the blessed hope that Paul talked about in (Titus 2:11-13).

Just imagine being chased by a vicious criminal who was stronger and faster in every area and no hope appears to be in sight. Suddenly, a strong defender and rescuer appear at your side. He has power the enemy cannot match and he assures you that He will help you. Oh what a relief that is!

In a sense, trials and the loss of loved ones are similar to such an enemy. All of us will be confronted by that enemy called death sooner or later. No one can escape. But God is more powerful that death and my friend Dorothy had faith and hoped in the Lord for strength. Scripture teaches "As the last enemy, death is to be brought to nothing." (1Corinthians 15:26)

Dorothy knew the difference between faith and hope and was able to act on both. Now hope is an action established on uncertainty and based on the idea of her faith. However, faith is based on the idea that whatever the consequences are, it is for the better.

Scriptures can help us understand how Jesus feels about death. Jesus reflected on the pain family members must feel when they lose loved ones by His experience with Mary and Martha when they learned of the death of their brother Lazarus. The Scripture account says, "Jesus gave way to tears" (John 11:33, 35) even though He knew something wonderful was about to take place. (John 11:3, 4). However, Martha didn't understand and gave up hope. But in four days the stone was rolled away and Jesus cried out "Lazarus, come on out!" And, guess what? "The man that had been dead came out" (John 11:43, 43). The account of the resurrection of Lazarus confirms that we can have hope in Jesus.

It was the hope focused on things not seen that motivates believers. The definition of hope encompasses the anticipation of a positive outcome regarding some ability, some situation, or person. Christian hope arise their relationship and trust in God. Genuine hope is having the firm assurance about unseen things. "For hope we have been saved, but hope that is seen is not hope; for who hopes for what he already sees? But if we hope for what we do not see, with perseverance we wait eagerly for it" (Romans 8:24-25-NASB). "Now faith is the assurance of things hoped for, the conviction of things not seen" (Hebrew 11:1-NASB).

If we hope to inherit God's kingdom, we all must have faith and hope. Though faith and hope work separately, they are parallels. The Bible teaches us that first we have hope and faith follows hope. Hope is the invisible root that faith grows out of. If there is no root, there is no tree, therefore if there is no hope faith cannot grow.

Faith and Hope

Throughout the years we have been provided with thousands of stories of God's people who faced death and other types of suffering with steadfast faith. The stories provide us with truth of the gospel and assurance that the gospel shines brightest during times of anguish. In addition, the stories offer us encouragement to persevere when problems come upon us. In the Bible, the suffering of agony, bondage, a bitter taste, corruption, enmity, and fear are associated with death (Hebrews 2:9, 14, 15; Acts 2:24; 1Corinthians 15:26, 53, 54). In each of these stories Jesus offers an alternative for our pains.

In the Scriptures, Jesus pleas to us to not only live well, but to die well. In Paul's letter to the Philippians, he wrote, "Your faith in the Lord and your service are like a sacrifice offered to him. And my own blood may have to be poured out with the sacrifice. If this happens, I will be glad and rejoice with you" (2:17).

Faith ultimately begins where the will of God is known. Hebrew 11:6, tells us that "Without faith it is impossible to please God." Faith begins with you and with me when the reality of God is realized. Ephesians 2:8, tells us that "For by grace you have been saved through faith and that not of yourselves; it is the gift of God."

A remarkable housekeeper had recognized me from the weekend stay my daughter and I had in downtown Atlanta. As we were preparing to leave the hotel and I stood at the front desk for checkout a young lady approached us. Before I could say anything she yelled out "Dr. Honey, "I have hoped and prayed to see you again so that I could share what God is doing in my life! I pray often since we prayed the last time you were here and since then I have seen remarkable changes in my life." She went on to say, "My daughter's life is changing and things have changed for the better on my job. I just wanted to say thank you for taking the time to pray with me." I was almost speechless and I assured her it wasn't me but it was her faith in the power of God.

During the few minutes I stood in line talking to her, we had the opportunity to discuss her relationship with Christ. The last summer when my daughter and I had stayed at the same hotel is when I first met this young lady. I remember her coming to clean my room and I was reading my Bible. I looked up and saw this sad eyed young person who looked hopeless. I asked her before leaving the room if everything was okay and she began crying. She shared that she had no relationship with Christ. Her children were out of control, and the pressures of working and attending college classes were stressful.

This young lady and her family have since then connected with a church in her community and she has come to have faith in Christ. She shared that her ability to cope with being a single parent, a student, and working full time has improved. I asked her to continue praying and to include me in her prays and she agreed.

If You Travail You Prevail

Israel ran into a major barrier on the way to the Promised Land. Amalek's people were there to cause trouble. This is Satan's way. When God has plans for you, you can rest assured that Satan will try to hinder it:

> *"Then came Amalek, fought with Israel in Rephidim. And Moses said to Joshua, Choose us some men and go out, fight with Amalek: Tomorrow I will stand on top of the hill with the rod of God in mine hand" (Exodus 17:8-9, KJV).*

Israel's battle with Amalek clearly explains the importance of prayer for believers during time of battle. God commanded Saul and the Israelites. The Lord Almighty said in 1 Samuel 15: 23, "I have noted what Amalek did to Israel in opposing them on the way when they came up out of Egypt. Now go and strike Amalek and devote to destruction all that they have. Do not spare them…" Moses, the committed leader of the nation on a journey, remained behind to pray. His reason was not because he was incapable of fighting, but he chose to do the most important duty which was to pray.

You Must Fight

Joshua and the men of war had to fight. Victory comes only through fighting. You must play your part before you expect God to do His. God is not some magician who works up instant miracles. Someone always does their part. Think about David and Goliath. David first had to pick up his stones then God approached the Giant with him. Joseph stood his ground and was jailed. God will add His touch only after each did their part. "For as the body without the spirit is dead, so faith without works is dead also" (James 2:26).

My grandson Calvin is an example of a fighter. His first love since he was a toddler was playing with and building airplanes. As he got older,

Jesus became his first love. Of course, airplanes held a strong second place in his heart. Today, Calvin attends Embry Riddle Aeronautical University in Florida. His strong faith in God allowed him to arrive at this point. Not because demons didn't attack from every angle.

It was prayer and perseverance that worked to help him obtain what God had already planned for him. I advise all children and adults to do as Calvin did, pray consistently, and work like there's no tomorrow. Your labor will not be in vain. God hears you. He knows the desires of your hearts. Just put Him first.

Calvin Cooper Jr.

My grandson and partner in prayer!
A young pilot, flying high for the Lord in the skies and on the ground!

Prayer is the Key

The battle rocked back and forth as Joshua and his men fought with Amalek: "And so it was when Moses held up his hand, that Israel prevailed; and when he let down his hand, Amalek prevailed." The battle swayed back and forth as his praying hands did.

Victory is not a physical experience; however victory does depend on your spiritual position which is aided by your physical contribution. You must make a physical contribution before the determination of your spiritual position.

A dear friend of mine, Dr. Ben Oruma, devoted a year of his campus life to mentoring young ministers on dealing with witchcraft and mystical practices. His message to them began with sharing one important spiritual law: The spiritual supersedes the physical such that whatever is determined in the spirit realm cannot be reversed in the physical" (Oruma, 2013).

Dr. Oruma stressed that a sickness that is induced in the spirit realm cannot be cured in the physical realm. Sometimes humans fail to realize that they cannot handle every ailment through medical treatment and all behaviors cannot be explained by psychology. Dr. Oruma plainly stressed that "You cannot counsel out what you're supposed to cast out!"

> *When Moses' hands grew tired, they took a stone and put it under him and he sat on it. Aaron and Hur held his hands up — one on one side, one on the other—so that his hands remained steady till sunset (Exodus 17:12).*

An explanation of why Israel prevailed when Moses's hands went up and why Amalek prevailed when they went down is very simple. There was a connection between the physical battle and the spiritual warfare. The parallel between the two suggest that when believers toil they will achieve victory.

Activating Your Faith

It is God's desire for us to have trust in what He said or says. Our faith requires total reliance on God, and believing in His ability to take care of us. Our struggles will end when we do our parts and understand that God wants to meet our needs. He activates the faith ability that He has already placed inside of us. When we enter into a trusting relationship with God we will be able to see His infinite glory. The gift of faith is more than we can ever touch or imagine.

What is faith and how do we activate it?

Faith is the assurance that what we hope for will happen; it gives us a guarantee about things we cannot see (Hebrews 11:1). Most of us are afraid of failure and we lack confidence in believing in something we cannot see. However, God's word will not only tell you what to do, it will give you power to do it. Your faith is increased as you grow in the understanding of God's word.

Unlike self-help books that give you instructions only, the Bible tells you exactly what to do and gives you the power to do it. Your faith is activated by the Word of God. His power is available to all believers who demand it. As believers, we are carriers of God's life, His authority, and His power therefore we can provoke God to manifest His power in our behalf. "If you can?" said Jesus. "Everything is possible for him who believes" (Mark 9:23). Our lives are significantly affected by whom or by what we put our confidence in. But those who build a strong faith and trust in the Lord shall realize the fulfillment of their needs.

Faith has very little to do with what we can accomplish but very much to do with whom we trust and believe in. Placing our faith in God and in the truth of the gospel we become victorious according to His perfect Will. Through faith we are aligned with God's plan for our lives. Impossibilities become possibilities through faith.

Jesus proved His love for us by dying on the cross for our sins and because of our faith in Him, we can boldly come into His presence (Ephesians 3:11-12). We also become more than conquerors in all things concerning us through Christ because He loved us enough to sacrifice Himself for us (Romans 8:37).

When we invoke God's help we must exercise our faith by believing that God has already done what we are asking Him to do. He is the author and the finisher of our faith, "And let us run with perseverance the race marked out for us, fixing our eyes on Jesus, the pioneer and perfecter of faith" (Hebrew 12:2 NIV). The foundation of activating our faith is authority. Authority represents the release of power. In order to have authority we must be under authority. God is that all mighty source power and authority and the deliverer of authority.

It is impossible to please God without faith. Therefore, anyone desiring to come to Him must believe that God exists. And, He will reward those who diligently seek Him (Hebrew 11:6). Our faith affirms that we truly believe in God's Omnipotence. He has the authority to do anything and through our belief and trust in him our faith is developed.

Developing Our Faith

Faith is developed through a learning process. We must first learn and believe that Jesus is the pioneer and perfecter of our faith (Hebrews 12:2a). We must place our trust in Him and build a relationship with Him through prayer. Building an intimate relationship with God will empower us to overcome any situation. This intimate relationship with Jesus gives us a revelation of the nature of God and of our rights as His children. We can depend on Him.

Faith is developed through hearing. "Faith comes by hearing and hearing by the Word of God" (Romans 10:17). The Word of God encourages us to clearly hear the voice of God. The Scripture also presents us with examples of individuals who triumphantly walked by faith during his or her trials. The stories told in the Bible about the challenges men and women faced and obtained victory by stepping out on faith is a reminder that faith conquers every issue that may arise in our lives.

The faith given to us by God deserves our praise. God promised us what he has already done for us in advance. He is therefore worthy of all of our praise. To grow in faith is also to grow in gratitude. Our praise represents a profound level of gratitude for who God is to us and the possibilities we have because of Him. Jesus said, "Everything is possible for Him who believes." (Mark 9:23) Growing in faith is extended by growing in praise.

The longer we live and the more we learn about Jesus we gain the awareness that none of life's limitations can stand in the way of God's power and ability. Nonetheless, the Lord expects us to be obedient and submissive to His Will. The greatest benefit we receive from our trials is that we are enabled to develop our faith. "For you know that your faith is tested, your endurance has a chance to grow" (James 1:3).

God said in James to consider it joy when we face trial. He did not say if, He said when. That tells us that surely we will face trials in this lifetime. But He went on to tell us, "Blessed is a man who perseveres under trials; for once he has been approved, he will receive the crown of life, which the Lord has promised to those who love Him" (James 1:12).

Every believer has a testimony of faith – a story of how he or she has experienced God working to make changes in their lives. Our testimonies can penetrate the hearts of others and provide them with some guidelines for building their own personal testimonies. The power of our testimony springs forth as we share with others the journey of our faith. Testimony about the works God has done in our lives through faith encourages those who seek Him. In his message to Timothy, Paul said "Therefore, do not be ashamed of the testimony about our Lord, nor of me his prisoner, but share in suffering for the gospel by the power of God" (2 Timothy 1:8, ESV).

Paul reminds that it's okay to share our love of God and His grace throughout encounters of our lives. Pray without ceasing and proclaim Him without shame. I pray words shared throughout the text will help someone find the faith, hope, and love of God that I cherish today. Turn your hardship into your Godship.

Chapter 11

The Glory of God

As you walk through life's journey, keep 2 Timothy 4:7-8 in mind, "I have fought the good fight, I have finished the race, I have kept the faith. Now there is in store for me the crown of righteousness, which the Lord, the righteous Judge, will award to me on that day — and not only to me, but also to all who have longed for his appearing.

One of the greatest rewards of faith is the joy we receive from looking at the unseen accomplishments that Jesus promised us and the expectation of the glories to come from having faith in Him. Through His promises we are assured to be like Him and to see Him if we are faithful unto death (2 Peter 1: 4). The stories in this book prove that no one is exempt from persecution. Jesus himself suffered more than any of us could ever imagine and yet He loved us enough to die for us. Take the leap of faith and start living. I think it's about time you made the decision to let faith be the driver and Jesus the guide.

Life comes packaged with its share of joy, sunshine, and pain. Every emotion imaginable exists throughout this journey. Through painful storms, I discovered a rainbow on the other side. These storms made me who I am today. And, allowed me to see that it's not about me but how to activate faith in God. What a blessing to witness storms pass over, clouds roll away, and the morning brings in sunshine.

The Lord gives each of us new days and opportunities to seek Him. God knows that we are not perfect beings and that we'll stumble from time to time. It is a blessing to know that He made provisions so we don't have to stumble alone. He's always near according to the Word of

God. So what if the darkness does come. Those of us who have faith in God are no longer walking blindly, "For we walk by faith, and not by sight" (2 Corinthians 5:7, ESV). All of us who have gone through a few storms can now rest assured that when it passes, we will be protected and kept safe in the arms of the greatest watchman ever born, Jesus.

The Lord stopped my heartache and He wiped away all of my tears. He even gave me a helpmate to share the gift of His love with. No matter what comes my way now, I have my Lord and my James. Together we are witnesses to His awesome power and we are growing daily in our faithfulness to Him. He is our comforter during the night and our sunshine in the morning. We arise daily to His marvelous creations. Our hearts sing Glory to the God of our salvation.

If you have been blessed to live a long life, I am sure you have seen many victories and faced many trials. You have laughed jubilantly and cried through much anguish and pain. You are and were not alone. You will continue to see good times and bad times because no one in his world is exempt. These are the realities of this world. Yet when we are facing situations that appear to be hopeless, when we can't understand why certain things happen, it is a blessing to know there is a solution to the problem in God.

> *Blessed be the God and Father of our Lord Jesus Christ, the Father of mercies and God of all comfort; who comforts us in all our affliction, so that we may be able to comfort those who are in any affliction, with the comfort with which we ourselves are comforted by God. 2 Cor. 1:3-4 ESV*

The Scripture refers to the Jesus as our Comforter in John 2:1 and the Holy Ghost as the Comforter in John 14:26. God is a mighty comforter and His presence gives provides a refuge for our hopelessness. God's love and grace pulls us out of the darkest gloom and releases our hearts from the bondage of pain. The Holy Spirit comforts the believer by picking us up when we fall. He has the ability to be there whenever you need him and God promised to never leave us comfortless, Hebrews 13:5. Whenever you need Him, He is near.

As we reflect on the stories in this book and study the Scriptures, we know that we are not the only ones to experience some form of pain or displeasure. We learned that many things took place in lives of many men and women in the Bible and the most drastic persecution was done to our savior Jesus Christ. Jesus promised to remove the headship of Satan over mankind Genesis 3:14-15. This solution, God and Jesus agreed upon before we were formed.

> *For our light affliction, which is but for a moment, worketh for us a far more exceeding and eternal weight of glory; while we look not at the things which are seen, but at the things which are not seen: for the things which are seen are temporal; but the things which are not seen are eternal (2Cor. 4:13-18).*

Everyone living will experience love and loses before leaving this earth. It is through losing that we gain the greatest appreciation of what we have. The rich who strive to be richer will realize that in the end money cannot buy the new soul that he or she needs, the poor will realize that the riches they long for are not worth the pain of having them, the bitter person will realize that the thing he or she was angry about doesn't even matter anymore, and the jealous will realize that the thing they were coveting is not worth the time they spent in anguish. The Word of God says, "For everything there is a season, and a time for every matter under heaven" (Eccles. 3:1, ESV). There is comfort in knowing that God holds our future. He knows the outcome for everyone. The greatest lesson to learn is how to seek Him.

> *And without faith it is impossible to lease him, for whoever would draw near to God must believe that he exists and that he rewards those who seek him (Hebrews 11:6, ESV).*

God will be there for you when everyone else is gone. He is there for us in the darkest hours and will guide you through the storm to the brightest light of your tomorrow. You can take comfort in knowing that you have an answer to your problems. So you've been tossed and your world seems upside down. It's not over. You had some hard days and nights but this too will pass. In God, there is rest for the weary. Jesus said:

> *Come to me, all you who labor and heavy laden, and I will give you rest. Take my yoke upon you, and learn from me, for I am*

gentle and lowly in heart, and you will find rest for your souls"
(Matthew 11:28-29, ESV).

So you've been knocked down a few times but you always get up. No matter how dark it has gotten, you have always found the light. You can believe in your heart that it was God protecting you and caring for you, nothing that you did. It was His love and His grace. God has never gone back on His word to us when He promised to never leave you or forsake you. He is the same yesterday, today and tomorrow. Understand that you will have trials and tribulations, but He is with you. Every lesson becomes a blessing to everyone who hears the message He has in it for you.

Whether young or old, rich, or poor everyone will experience something in life that he or she has no control over. Having faith in God brings hope. The profound truth is that Jesus is the way, and the only way. There is salvation in no one else and every knee shall bow and every tongue shall confess allegiance to Him regardless of age, race, status or place. So, just as I had to learn through my dark and gloomy days, you can also. He is always there. Just have faith and believe.

The Glory of God!

To the broken men, God made you strong and powerful. Occasionally, you are robed of the opportunity to learn how to love and of being guided by a strong man but God sent excellent mothers to love and nurture you until you can stand on your own. Sometimes along the way you run in to what I call *Life's Traffic Jams.* These are traps Satan sets to turn you from the direction God wants you to go in. But be strong because God occasionally sends a good woman into your life to love you and to be your friend. She is good source of support, however, the greatest source of your strength can only be found through your faith in God.

To the women of little faith, no matter what sorrows and despair life has brought you, don't give up. Joy comes in the morning. Joy is at end of every teardrop, ever broken relationship, every hour of abuse, and every moment of low self-esteem. You are special to God. Sometimes life sends you unfortunate situations which shatter your dreams and leaves you feeling unloved and hopeless. However, God occasionally sends a messenger in the form of a friend or a mate to wrap their loving arms around you and give you the well needed love and support you long for. Don't be discouraged. Use your experiences to bless God by empowering other women and girls so that they may be able to resist the Devil's wiles. The Lord is your strength and your redeemer.

To the heartbroken and frightened children, both male and female, you are loved by God. A very special thanks to Him that one day, you will emerge as strong and courageous parents and leaders. Do not give up or give in when Satan attacks you through the cruelty of others. You will sometimes be discriminated against over your appearance, your weight, and your character, but do not allow those things or peer pressures determine who you are. God has already made provisions for you and He is your BFF. No friend could ever be closer and no one will ever love you better than Jesus. Occasionally, He will send a strong arm to embrace you and help keep you feel safe. But no experience will ever replace the one of spending time with Him. Through faith in Christ, you will receive all of the power and strength necessary to survive in this world.

To the Christian ministers, evangelist, and missionary workers who feel like they've exhausted their efforts trying to persuade unbelievers to follow Christ – don't quit! You may have even encountered being disrespected and unappreciated. Yes, the burdens of being an effective spiritual leader are heavy. Sometimes, confusion may have you ready to give up on your charge. But, you must not quit. God's faithfulness has brought you this far. He will carry you to the finish line. Just remember, God's glory is constant and you have seen it manifested before in your own life and others. Just remember that you have the glory of the Lord as your rear guard (Isaiah 58:6-8).

No matter what sorrows life has brought to us, the Lord God is the author and the finisher of our faith. He has the power to bring an end to the darkness and turn on the light of joy in our lives. You may be the product of an unmarried couple or come from a broken home. Yet, this doesn't determine your worth. You may come from generations of dysfunctional people. Yet, this does not determine who you are. You may have been raped, beaten, or abused. Yet, these tragic circumstances do not determine who you are. Who you are in Christ determines who you are in life. Do not allow losses and disappointments encountered rob you of the joys that having faith in God can bring. I encourage you to activate your faith "and my God will meet all of your needs according to the riches of His glory in Christ Jesus" (Philippians 4:19, NIV).

An Invitation to Live in His Glory

Glory to God in the highest! How excellent is your name, Oh Lord! The Hebrew word for "glory" is Kabod; it means weight. Glory is manifested and revealed in God's love for us (1 John 4:16).

I am praising God right now! There is one more voice I desire to hear praising Him too and that is yours! God is concerned about you. He is interested in your praise. He is interested in having a relationship with every man, woman, and child under the sound of His voice. His love is the same today as it was for those men and women discussed in this book and those mentioned in the Bible.

I substituted "gloom" with "glitz" believing that earthly things could bring me joy and failed. But God showed me His glory. Glory that's available to you also. The Lord has released me from the bondage of my past, given me strength for today, and through faith in Him I have hope for tomorrow. The Lord Jesus who is called the brightness of God's glory made the ultimate sacrifice for you and for me (Hebrew 1:3). On that note, I again say, "*Glory to God!*"